GOD'S CO-WORKERS

God's Co-Workers
'Your Importance to God'

Clyde W. Rathwick

Exposition Press of Florida, Inc.   Pompano Beach, Florida

FIRST EDITION 1-86

ISBN 0-682-40223-0

Printed in the United States of America

Gift
Editorial

DEDICATION

Dedicated to the glory of God and to the members of the Tower Class of Trinity-First United Methodist Church of El Paso, Texas who encouraged me to compile this work.

Contents

Preface

It has been stated that the total sum and substance of one's knowledge lies in direct proportion to what one has seen, read and heard. That knowledge is also dependent upon one's powers of comprehension and upon the open mindfulness with which one approaches a given subject or line of inquiry. Of course, one should not embark upon a line of inquiry into any given subject if he lacks the courage to pursue it to its ultimate conclusion, no matter where it might lead. The subject matter contained herein has been approached from a Christian viewpoint, using the Judeo-Christian Scriptures as a point of reference. This writing, insofar as it pertains to ethical and moral laws, is not to be narrowly interpreted as being applicable only to the Christian, but to men of all faiths and of good will. This book does not apply to those whose dogma and rituals do not contain the essence of a religion because of what they do and teach which downgrades the quality of life rather than lifting it to its highest values.

The writings of many theologians, philosophers, sociologists, church leaders and lay authors as well as others dealing in the subject matter of this book have been the focal point of my studies throughout my adult life. I have also searched the Scriptures, not only those which pertain to Christianity, but also those which pertain to other faiths and which are and have been followed by our brethren in the search for the ultimate meaning and purpose of this life.

The foregoing statements are not to be interpreted as having been made in an attitude of boasting, for that was not my purpose, but they are intended to explain why, throughout this book, there may be imparted a certain wisdom that is not of my own mind. It is, therefore, stipulated that some of what has been written in this book may be the product of other minds. The material contained herein has been gleaned from lectures which I have delivered over the years, and to attempt to now acknowledge each and every source of information would require the rereading of an entire lifetime of studies. At the time the lectures were given, no thought of ever having them compiled into a book was considered. However, far too many persons have encouraged me to do just that, and thus this writing. Acknowledgment is therefore given to those great thinkers of the past whose thoughts and words may appear herein either in pure or in hybrid form. In some cases their words, which were intended to lead their students to a given conclusion, may have been used in this book to arrive at a different conclusion. If I have done any harm to their works and thoughts, it was not intended.

There may also appear throughout this book certain repetitions; however, this was intended. It was done for the convenience of the reader and to use any less effective wording could not do justice to the subject under discussion. This was held to a minimum.

It is my sincere desire to impart what has been revealed to me and what I have learned. I am aware that there are many who are far more learned than I who will take exception to what is said in the pages that follow. Nevertheless, it is my belief that what I have written will prove to be a blessing to many who read this book with an open mind, and will result in the reader having obtained additional knowledge to aid him in his own quest to find the ultimate meaning to his life and to his net worth to God. It is my sincere hope that this book will not result in the reader believing that all that is important is the salvation of one's own personal soul, to the exclusion of the spiritual needs of his brethren.

Complete acceptance of what is said herein is neither contemplated nor expected. As long as men and women are free thinkers, ideas will differ and different conclusions will be drawn from the reading of any written word. In addition, conviction in some is far more deeply rooted than in others, and this is rightfully so. But there are some truths which are not subject to further inquiry, nor should they be subjected to further discussion or disagreement. These I am certain will be recognized by any man who professes faith in God.

GOD'S CO-WORKERS

I

Faith Versus Belief

Many people today are having difficulty in maintaining their beliefs and their faith in the face of our rapidly changing world. They are asking, "How can we keep our faith in view of the miracles of modern science, including heart transplants, the creation of life in test tubes, the space program and the walk on the moon? If intelligent life is found to exist on other planets, will man's net worth to God be diminished?" With each new social problem including excessive permissiveness of sex, dope addiction, dishonesty and the lowering of our ethical and moral standards the doubt continues to mount.

This questioning of faith is due, in part, to the fact that most people simply to do not understand the meaning of the word "faith". Although the word "faith" has common usage, few understand its exact connotation.

In Hebrews faith is defined as follows: "Now faith is the substance of things hoped for, the evidence of things not seen. Through faith we understand that the worlds were formed by the word of God. Without faith it is impossible to please Him, for he that cometh to God must believe that He is, and that He is a rewarder of them that diligently seek Him."

Webster defines faith as "belief in God, or the like, or in a practical religious sense, trust in God." Thus, belief and trust form a part of the definition of faith.

Trust is the assumed reliance in another's integrity or veracity. Trust is a simple belief in justice and reflects complete confidence in another person or in a deity. To have trust one must have a belief in some outside influence in which one can have faith and in which one can believe.

Belief is the state of mind of one who believes. To believe a thing, one must have confidence in it, he must have a conviction of truth. He must believe in its credibility, its reliance, and its integrity.

What is truth? A belief is true *not because it agrees with fact* but because it agrees, that is to say, harmonizes, in direct proportion to the body of knowledge that we possess. Both savage and civilized man respond when an old truth is rejected and a new truth declared. It is because the new truth coheres better with the increased knowledge and experiences that we possess,

1

than does the rejected truth. Whenever we declare that a thing is true we are, in fact, evaluating it. Just as we evaluate certain things as good or bad, pleasant or unpleasant, beautiful or ugly, so we evaluate the things called propositions or beliefs as true or false. When an individual declares a belief to be "true," it means that the belief, insofar as it is held by him, fits in with the sum total of his interests, experience, and knowledge. Sometimes a person will declare a thing to be true and subsequently retract that belief. This means that in the course of time the truth has proved to be useless and is now rejected and called false.

Most truths are the result of social intercourse after which they are accepted by the group or society to which the person is exposed. For example, Christ said, "I am the truth." The Jews as a group do not accept this, based on their knowledge. They do not accept it as a truth. The Christian community accepts the statement at its face value and to them it is a truth. All truth valuations are corrected and altered under influence of the society until certain beliefs are accepted as generally true. A truth expressed and maintained by only one person will not be accepted by the group as a truth if the group believes otherwise, and it cannot be said to be a truth if it remains in that state. A person who alone holds to what he calls a truth is damned by his brothers if his truth disagrees with the opinion of the group. An example of this is an atheist in a Christian world. A truth, to gain recognition as a truth, depends to a large degree *not on knowledge, but also on acceptance by a large majority of the group and need not have universal acceptance.* The truth regarding the existence of God becomes true when we become convinced that we have knowledge of Him and this belief is not held alone, but by many.

It is important that one be able to distinguish between the use of the word "belief" and the word "faith." Although they are often used interchangeably, they do not have exactly the same parallel, for belief may or may not imply that the person who believes is certain of his beliefs. He may have a feeling of certainty, yet there remains a shadow of a doubt. The fact that one states that he believes in a thing does not rule out uncertainties. *However, faith, when used in a religious or scriptural sense, always means a state of absolute, a state of being absolutely certain, even though there is no evidence or proof.*

Faith, then, when used in a religious sense, can be said to mean complete belief in God's promises, total allegiance to His teachings, and complete confidence in His saving grace even though some of the dogma may be open to question or suspicion and cannot be fully explained. Trust and belief are subject to qualification, but faith is absolute.

Paul expresses his faith in Romans: "For I am persuaded, that neither death, nor life, nor angels, nor principalities, nor powers, nor things present, nor things to come, nor height, nor depth, nor any other creature, shall be able to separate us from the love of God, which is in Christ Jesus our Lord."

Here is an expression of absolute faith. It is absolute, and nothing, Paul says, can persuade him otherwise.

Faith, when sincere, comes from the heart, which it sanctifies, and works by love to overcome the temptations of this world. In Galatians we read, "But faith which worketh by love." In Acts we read, "To open their eyes, and to turn them from darkness to light, and from the power of Satan unto God, that they may receive forgiveness of sins, and inheritance among them which are sanctifed by faith," In I John we read, "for whatsoever is born of God overcometh the world, and this is the victory that overcometh the world by faith."

Christians are justified by faith, also they are purified by faith, walk by it, and have access to God through it. In Romans we read, "Therefore we conlcude that a man is justified by faith without deeds of law," and in Acts, "And put no difference between us and them, purifying their hearts by faith," and in II Corinthians, "For we walk by faith, not by sight."

How do we recognize, need, and justify having faith? We generally know when we wish to ask a question and when we wish to make a statement. There is a feeling that we have when we wish to express one or the other. There is also a distinct feeling between the sensations of faith and doubt. Doubt is an uneasy and dissatisfied state from which we struggle to free ourselves and pass into a state of belief which is a calm and satisfactory state which most of us seek and thereafter we do not wish to change our feelings to something else. On the contrary, we cling tenaciously, not merely to believing, but to believing in just what we do believe.

The irritation of doubt causes a struggle to attain a state of belief. The irritation of doubt is the motivating factor in our struggle to attain belief. We don't like the feeling of uncertainty. Our beliefs should be such as may truly guide our actions so as to satisfy our desires, and this make us reject every belief which does not seem to have been formed so as to put us in a peaceful state of mind. With doubt, therefore, the struggle begins, and with the cessation of doubt the struggle ends. *Thus the object of seeking faith is to bring about a settlement of inner conflict.* We may well fancy that we do not seek a mere resolution of the inner conflict, but that we seek the truth. But, put this fancy to test, and it proves groundless, for as soon as a firm belief is reached and we are entirely satisfied we will cling to that belief, whether it be true or false.

Whenever a man removes all doubt from his mind and then refuses to waver from that position, even though it may be in error, it is an entirely desirable state in which to live. It cannot be denied by anyone that a steady and immovable faith yields great peace of mind. Let us assume that death is the final act and there is nothing beyond the grave. No harm can come from one believing that when he dies he will go straight to heaven if he fulfills certain simple observations in this life, for even if his belief is faulty he will in no way ever experience disappointment *having no awareness of the rightness or wrongness of his beliefs.* If this is the way the man wants to believe, can anything be said against his doing so? If we do so, it would be only to admit that his beliefs are not the same as ours, which may themselves be faulty. Thus, faith brings inner peace, and this is a desirable state.

Absolute faith, though not subject to further inquiry, should not, however, preclude the entertainment of new ideas and knowledge. Faith is difficult for many to attain, for although many loudly proclaim absolute faith, they have a fear that some new knowledge or scientific event might alter that faith. This attitude is, of itself, destructive, for it tends to weaken, not strengthen, one's faith, and precludes the receipt of knowledge which has been promised to man by Christ when he said, "But the comforter, which is the Holy Ghost, whom the Father will send in my name, He shall teach you all things, and I have yet many things to say to you, but you cannot bear them now, however, the comforter will guide you unto all truth." And in Luke we read, "For there is nothing covered, that shall not be revealed, neither hid, that shall not be known."

In the broadest sense, faith means steadfastness in beliefs, *not blind acceptance*, and one should not fear new knowledge. Many, however, adopt a more comfortable course and cling to the beliefs they already hold, for they do not want to be troubled with new ideas, nor do they wish to face the necessity of revising their habits of thought.

They will accept only that which is compatible with what they already believe and will regard any new knowledge with hostility and suspicion, and in many cases, when confronted with new knowledge, will refuse to even entertain it, and when they do, they will automatically brand the new information as false or refuse to give it to any recognition. This is why our missionaries find it so difficult to convert other religiouns to Christianity. They are comfortable in their beliefs and do not wish to disturb their inner feelings.

The refusal to consider new information is an admission of little faith. For so long as one feels loss of faith, it is not absolute. For example, a person of absolute faith will admit that there is no scientific evidence for or against the belief in the existence of God or of human immortality, but he knows that he is justified in believing that there is a God and that men are immortal. These beliefs are the deepest cravings of man, and are the ultimate goal of Christianity. Absolute faith in God should be our highest aim, but this can be accomplished *only when we have faith in our own convictions of faith.*

Faith is not based on reason and logic, but on things not seen. This is of itself productive of inner conflicts which cease only when the existence of God is accepted on faith. Anyone who is moved by faith is conscious of an inner miracle. At first he finds that his faith is in conflict with reason. Then, as time passes, he becomes aware of the fact that faith reduces all principles of logic, understanding, and scientific inquiry to a state of nonrecognition.

Faith gives to the believer a determination to believe in that which is unbelievable, in that which is contrary to logic, and in that which surpasses all human understanding. It can be seen that faith is truly an inner miracle, and once achieved, dissolves all inner conflicts into inner peace. Thereafter, those who have found faith are no longer slaves to the old-age question, "Is there a God?", for he knows that there is a God. Persons who truly arrive at a state of complete faith are fortunate indeed, for they are the recipients of a living miracle.

One of the miracles of faith is that one almost immediately finds himself involved in the problems of life. He is alive with a new awareness of humanity. He feels compassion for his fellow man, and waves of sadness sweep over him as he witnesses the terrible agonies that mankind endures in his struggle against the forces of evil. Anyone who hears about human suffering and does not suffer a little himself, if he feels no compassion, no heartache, then that person is of little faith. If one does experience these emotions and then acts to give what relief he can, whenever possible and practicable, then he has faith and his acts will strengthen that faith. However, one must guard against the possibility that his faith in God might become subordinated to his compassion for his fellow man. If one goes too far in the direction of service to one's fellow man he risks loss of faith in God, for in his compassion he tends to blame God for whatever happens and in some cases even becomes resentful and embittered, for his comprehension of God's will is faulty. He must stand upon his faith. *Love of fellow man and love of God must always be kept in balance.* Today we find the church deeply involved in this struggle, love of man or love of God.

There are some who believe that the church should be used as an agency for social control and that religion should be primarily an institution for the promotion of ethical ideals and human welfare. They believe that the church ought to divest itself as much as possible of dogma and supernaturalism and concern itself mainly with the promotion of ethical values and the humanities.

Some believe that we should make concessions to science but retain a firm belief in a personal God and in the immortality of the soul. They also maintain that ethical values will follow as a matter of course.

Still others believe that religion should be based on service to mankind, rather than to the worship of God. They are agnostics. They believe in the supreme worth of man. That man is the cause of all evil, that he should bear the full responsibility and that he should not try to shove the blame off onto the shoulders of some God.

Out of these struggles there is a definite trend towards socialization and towards the belief that the church should assist in meeting social problems. They agree that the worship of God should be retained, but believe that it should be interwoven into the social ethics, that worship should run as an undercurrent rather than as the mainstream religion.

Still others believe that the church should devote its time, energies, and wealth solely to the teachings of God's word. It should utilize the Bible as the basis for its teachings and to substantiate its dogma. It should utilize only such writings and teachings of men as are compatible with biblical doctrine. It should utilize biblical doctrine in its teachings as to how man should conduct himself, one to another. Having done so, the church should then abide by its mandate to teach unto all the world the word of God.

Church members, having learned from her, should then go out into the world and serve man in the name of God, such service to be in accord with church and biblical doctrine. Having learned from the church, we should do our good works outside the church through organizations established by men for such purposes, the same as does the medical student. After having his training, he goes forth to practice medicine among men.

Church organizations should be utilized for God and men's organizations for men. It should be borne in mind that Christ did not set forth a single formula as to how men should serve and love his fellow man, *but He simply said that he should.* He put forward no schemes, He recommended no forms of government, He did not teach utopia, communism, or democratic forms of government. He recommended no organizations that we should support. He put forward no tax formulas for the sharing of wealth, no poverty programs, nothing. For He knew that if man truly loved God he would follow His word and by nature would do that which was expected of him in relation to his fellow man. He did not interweave the church with wordly organizations, but He kept the word of God separate and different. He taught the word of God and man is to fulfill the word. The church should do no less.

If a man truly loves God, then God abides in him and he cannot do other than good deeds. It is an impossibility to do otherwise.

We are all involved in these struggle of ideologies. We are involved in the race struggle, social problems, poverty problems, in world problems and all the rest, yet it is through these struggle that we draw our convictions which, if we retain our faith in God, will in the final analysis strengthen that faith. This surely must be so or we would disintegrate and regress into the dark ages. Love of God and love of man must be kept in balance.

At one time or another all of us will encounter Christ, and we will be called on to make a decision, a declaration of faith, and after having done so, to thereafter (to use a modern expression) "Keep the faith, baby." This is all important, for we must not become so involved and embroiled in the humanities that *we lose sight of our trust in God and place our trust in ourselves*, and thus lose our faith, and therefore our very lives.

To indulge in a search for absolute proof of the existence of God so as to have faith in Him is an exercise in futility. It is true some divine truths are attainable by human reason, but others altogether surpass the power of human reason and lie beyond our comprehension. We must realize that we cannot prove the existence of God by scientific inquiry or by intellectual discourse. Then, what is left? The answer is faith.

II

Love

The word "charity" is defined in the dictionary as: "Charity; Christian love. Divine love for man. Act of loving all men as brothers because they are sons of God. Good will to the poor and the suffering, almsgiving, public provision for the relief of the poor. Lenience in judging men and their actions." Love and charity are synonymous. In the King James Version, I Corinthians reads as follows: "And now abideth faith, hope, charity, these three; but the greatest of these is charity." The Revised Standard Version reads as follows: "So faith, hope, love abide, these three; but the greatest of these is love."

The word "love" has many different meanings to different persons. Popular definitions may be grouped under three general meanings. One is the desire to possess and enjoy some value! A person might say, "I love ice cream." This is a selfish type of love and seems to be the major element in much of the shallow, romantic love that is predominant in movies, popular songs, novels, and magazines. A higher form of the value of love is found in the search for the good, the true, and the beautiful.

The second group of meanings centers in friendly relationships of persons. It is the opposite of ill will and hatred. It includes natural affection for the family, the nobler aspects of romantic love, and love of neighbor. This is a mixture of self-reward and concern for others.

The third and higher meaning of love is the genuine concern for the welfare of others, such as the love of a mother for her child, or the sacrifice of a martyr. John writes "Greater love has no man than this, that a man lay down his life for his friends."

Loving and liking are not the same. One can like a person but not love him. He can also love a person but not like him. Many children, for example, love their parents but do not particularly like them. Also, it has been said that man cannot love an inanimate object, he can only like them, but he can love animate objects, because they are capable of returning that love and affection.

Christian love is not easy, for we are extolled to love our enemies, to do good to other people, to lend to others, to avoid making judgments about others, to not condemn others, to forgive your fellow man, and to give to those who are in need. At the same time, we are told not to expect any benefits, rewards, or praise as a result of our acts of love, or else we do not act out of love. We are to expect nothing in return, but are to give freely of ourselves. We know that to love is right and good, and to hate is wrong and evil, but it is not easy to always love, to suppress our feelings of dislike for others, to love those who have wronged us. It takes great strength and conviction to love as a Christian ought to love.

Luke records that Jesus said, "But love your enemies, and do good, and lend, expecting nothing in return, and your reward will be great and you will be sons of the Most High; for He is kind to the ungrateful and the selfish. Be merciful, even as your Father is merciful." Love cannot be commanded or created by self-discipline, but comes through us from God because God's love has been poured into our hearts through the Holy Spirit which has been given to us."

If we thought our friends loved us only because of what we could do for them, we would not have a high regard for their love. It is only when we have knowledge that people love us for what we are without feeling that they seek reward, that we experience the warm glow of true love. *To love, or to be loved for reward, dilutes the meaning of the word "love" to a point where it is no longer worthy of being referred to as love.*

Love for the sake of reward is really a form of self-love. Those who are motivated by hope of reward actually defraud themselves. They miss one of the noblest experiences of life, to love and to be loved.

When are are hurt by another, one of the first sensations is that of getting even and we find comfort in the belief that "he will get his, someday." Jesus rejected this reaction to hurts and denied that old law of "an eye for an eye, a tooth for a tooth," and substituted, therefore, the doctrine of brotherly love and forgiveness. Romans says, "Bless those who persecute you; bless and do not curse them. Rejoice with those who rejoice, weep with those who weep. Live in harmony with one another; do not be haughty, but associate with the lowly, never be conceited. Repay no one evil for evil, but take thought of what is noble in the sight of all."

It is a natural thing for us to strike back at those who hurt us. How can we love our enemies? Well, *divine love does not claim to be natural, it is supernatural.* When we realize that Christ came into the world to save sinners, His enemies, the anti-God pagans, and that He laid His life down for them, then we realize the scope of divine love. When we realize that our enemies are loved by God, how can we hate them, and at the same time cherish His love for us? When this realization comes, we are amazed to find that we do not hate our enemies and will develop a desire to help them, to actually love them. This is the miracle of divine love.

Just how far are we to go in loving our enemies and our neighbor? How far should we go in forgiving those who trespass against us? Jesus gave us the answer to this when He said, "You shall love your neighbor as yourself." Just how far does one go in loving one's self? This can become an evil in itself, for excessive self-love is a selfish thing and has no place in divine love. The best guideline to follow is to determine your relationship to God, to engage in self-analysis and self-evaluations, being perfectly honest with yourself, and then ask yourself, "If I have all these shortcomings, if I commit all the wrongs that I do, if I have caused so many tears to flow in others, if I hurt others, if I have made so many enemies, how is it possible that God can love me?" Then, when you realize that God really does love you in spite of all your shortcomings, *not because of your goodness, but in spite of your weaknesses*, then the meaning of divine love becomes clear and it becomes a wondrous thing. Come to this realization and you will find that you are capable of likewise loving your enemies, for if God abides in you, and you in him, then a spark of the divine is in you and you are capable of divine love and not just natural love.

Jesus taught, "As the Father has loved me, so I have loved you, abide in my love; and this is my commandment, that you love one another as I have loved you."

Our guidelines are also spelled out in Ephesians, "Let all bitterness and wrath and anger and clamor and slander be put away from you, with all malice, and be kind to one another, tenderhearted, forgiving one another, as God in Christ forgave you. Therefore be imitators of God, as beloved children. And walk in love, as Christ loved us and gave Himself up for us."

These are hard guidelines and it is doubtful if any of us can say that we abide fully by these instructions, but this is not the point. All that God requires is that we earnestly strive to abide by them. *It is the struggle that we wage to abide that is important*. We are not gods, but humans, and we fail over and over in our attempts to abide by our instructions. Nevertheless, we must try with earnest desire, and if we do this then God will love us even though we fail through human weakness in our endeavor. It is the struggle that we wage, not necessarily the success we have, that forms the basis for judgment.

We often hear the expression "Love is blind." Love is not blind, but instead it opens our eyes and we see good in people whom we formerly thought evil. Love enables us to look deeper than one's skin, and the beauty that we find there cannot be seen by anyone who does not love. Love opens our eyes to people all about us and we are sometimes amazed at how blind we were when we did not love them, and those we thought ugly are beautiful, those we did not like are likeable, those we thought selfish are generous, those we thought withdrawn were merely lonely, those we thought harsh were merely covering their softness for fear of further hurt. Love opens your eyes and enables us to really look at the people with whom we are in contact and see them for the first time as they truly are. Love is not blind, but loves sees clearly and distinctly as we never saw before.

You are all familiar with the song, "What the World Needs Now is Love, Sweet Love, not just for some, but for everyone." Well, the world doesn't need love, for love abounds; it flows from God and engulfs the whole world. What the world needs now is people who will open their eyes and see the love that is available for them, and they will discover that there is so much love that they cnanot use it all, and then take the excess and shower it upon their fellow men. *The world does not need love, it needs men and women who will and can love.* There is plenty of love if we will but take it and share it. What the world needs now is people who will love and be loved— that's all it needs!

We see bumper stickers and signs and printed slogans on walls and buildings saying one word, "Love." It is an expression of desire, of hope, of dreams, but it is also an expression of those who do not know true love. One does not love humanity by removing oneself from it, one does not love by forming groups and by giving oneself all kinds of titles and then engaging in self-pleasures by saying, "Aren't we the great lovers. We will love one another, but we will not share it with the world. Who needs the world? Let's cop out and sit around all the day long and love one another. Let's become problems to the local communities; let's break the hearts of our parents; let's make the older generation worry about the future and what will happen to us. Above all, we shall let all others boil in their own stew, while we love one another. We will keep our love among ourselves, sharing with no one, hurting with no one, weeping with no one, dreaming with no one, aiding no one. To Hell with the world. Let's love. Love!" *They don't know the meaning of the word*! It is a farce and they are frauds, without understanding, for they profess to love Christ and in their self-centeredness believe that that is all there is to it, their own selfish salvation. But Christ came into the world, He worked among men; He suffered with them, not apart from them; He touched them; He healed them; He loved them. He did not take his followers into the wilderness aside and apart from the world, but threw them into the middle of life where they were persecuted and martyred; they knew love, they knew how to love. One knows the greatest meaning of love when he works with people, among them for what they are—other humans who struggle to alter the world, to make this a better place to live. This is love, working with men, among men so that all might benefit and know the meaning of love of God and the abundance of it. Not among ourselves, hoping to attract it all to ourselves to the exclusion of the whole world!

World history reveals that civilizations fell because of corruption, dishonesty, and from the search for kicks. But the greatest contributor to their downfall were the ones who did not know how to love, who ran away, who would not stand their ground, who professed a love of God, but rather than stand and fight they fled, physically, into the hills, and mentally into the shelter of accepting the politics they did not like, of accepitng that which downgraded their moral standards, by excusing crime, dope use, and all the rest, by placing the blame upon the society, by permitting youth to do their thing, be it productive or not. Well, *Love does not run—it stands fast.* Love does not yield to evil pressures, but resists that which is evil with all its might. Love does not whimper, love acts. To be of value it must move among men or else it will wither and die. Softness, yielding, whimpering, sniveling— these are not the marks of love. If you love your children, you will stand fast and not mistake weakness for strength. Love cannot retreat but it must stand fast or else you yourself will not be loved. Of this you may be assured—retreat and you will not be loved, but despised because of your weakness!

Love is defined in the Bible in I Corinthians in this way, "And if I have prophetic powers, and understand all mysteries and all knowledge, and if I have all faith, so as to remove mountains, but have not love, I am nothing. If I give away all I have and if I deliver my body to be burned, but have not loved, I gain nothing. Love is patient and kind, love is not jealous or boastful; it is not arrogant or rude. Love does not insist on its own way; it is not irritable or resentful; it does not rejoice at wrong, but rejoices in right. Love bears all things, endures all things. Love never ends."

In Romans we read, "Let love be genuine, hate what is evil, hold fast to what is good, love one another with brotherly affection; outdo one another in showing honor. Love does no wrong to a neighbor; therefore, love is the fulfilling of the law." Peter: "Above all hold unfailing your love for one another, since love covers a multitude of sins."

John wrote: "He who loves his brother abides in the light, and in it there is no cause for stumbling. Do not love the world or the things in the world. If anyone love the world, love for the Father is not in him. He who does not love remains in death. Anyone who hates his brother is a murderer, and you know that no murderer has eternal life abiding in him. Let us not love in word or speech but in deed and in truth. Beloved, let us love one another, for love is of God, and he who loves is born of God and knows God. He who does not love does not know God; for God is love. In this, the love of God was made manifest among us, that God sent his only son into the world, so that we might live through him. So we know and believe the love God has for us. God is love, and he who abides in love abides in God and God abides in him. There is no fear in love, but perfect love casts out fear. For fear has to do with punishment, and he who fears is not perfected in love. We love, because He first loved us." These are some of the most beautiful passages in the Bible. They are not to be merely read, but are to be read thoughtfully so that we can abide by the mandate that Christ gave to us, "That you love one another as I have loved you."

What the world needs now is men and women who will take the abundance of love that God showers upon the world and share it with their fellows. This is what the world needs now, and nothing more.

III

Moral Order

Peter writes, relating to Paul's teachings, "So also our beloved brother Paul wrote to you according to the wisdom given him, speaking as he does in all of his letters. There are some things in them hard to understand, which the ignorant and unstable twist to their own destruction, as they do the other scriptures." In the broadest sense, "morals" means man's relationship with God, or good and evil. "Ethics" means man's relationship to man, or right or wrong acts. For example, the first four of the Ten Commandments deal with man's relationship with God, but the remaining six deal with man's relationship with man. In addition, Christ said, "Thou shalt love the Lord your God with all your heart, and with all your soul, and with all your mind. This is the great and first commandment. And a second is like it, you shall love your neighbor as yourself. On these two commandments depend all the law and the prophets." The first part pertained to God, and the second part to man.

"Moral order" always leads to considerable debate when one tries to equate morals to nature and the universe. The quarrels that arise out of what is moral and what is immoral, and absolutes pertaining thereto, will probably never be resolved to anyone's complete satisfaction, because the matter of conscience always enters into such debates, and peoples' consciences are not the same. Yet there is in each of us a small voice that tells us when we do a right thing and when we do a wrong thing, and it will not be hushed, only buried beneath excuses and self-justification.

A society without ethical laws is impossible and, unless those who are associated with it agree to observe certain rules of conduct towards one another, it cannot exist for long. Its stability depends upon the steadfastness with which they abide by the agreement, and whenever they waver, then the forces that bind it together will weaken, and in many cases the society is destroyed. Men must establish ethical laws and must agree to use the force of the body as a whole against those who violate the rules, and in favor of those who abide by them, although many of our recent court decisions appear to ignore these basic, fundamental rules. This set of rules, with their system of rewards and punishments, becomes known as justice when one

12

is punished when the rules are breached, and is called a miscarriage of justice when one is not punished and the society, as a whole, suffers.

But ethical justice must always have a system of balances, for wrong acts done involuntarily, or with just cause, must be weighed against willful intent, and for unjust purposes; on other words, *a wrong act does not always merit punishment, nor does a good act always merit reward.* A good exmaple of this is murder. If the law says one shall not murder and then some-one does so, the public tends to set up a sort of compromise between themselves and the courts to provide a sanctuary for the guilty, as in the case of the so-called unwritten law. Thus, the concept of punishment or reward, according to acts, compromise itself into punishment or reward, according to motives, or just desserts.

Any attempt to equate this to nature encounters difficulty, for if there is one thing that is clear it is that neither obedience nor disobedience in the animal world results in reward or punishment, because it is admittedly impossible for the lower orders of life to deserve or merit anything that happens to them. When the lion slays the deer, can it be said that the deer got its just desserts? Or when a lion is gored to death on the horns of a bull, did he got his just desserts when nature herself decreed that he shall kill to eat? Thus, good and evil in nature equates itself to what the human mind conceives to be good or evil.

Thoughtful men have long moralized over and pondered the fact that violators of ethical and moral laws constantly escape the punishment they deserve, or in the least, they are not punished as we think they ought to be, that by mere legal maneuvering the guilty escape punishment while the innocent suffer, that the wicked flourish while the righteous beg, that in the realm of nature ignorance appears to be punished just as severely as willful wrong, and that thousands of innocents suffer from crime, physically and economically, both directly and indirectly, through taxes required to ap-prehend, protect against, convict and house the guilty, while men of good will are in need of daily bread. One thing is certain—the world is full of pain and sorrow and grief, and evil falls, like the rain, upon both the just and unjust, and we cannot explain it away by merely saying that there is nothing good or bad but thinking makes it so, because sooner or later reality rears its ugly head and demands recognition!

We can, of course, take the position that nothing in the world is as good or as bad as it could be, and we all have from time to time experienced both good and evil in the extremes. In addition, we all know that by our acts and by the acts of others, evil can be increased or decreased, and by the same token, good can also be increased or decreased, and strangely enough, for each individual it is a matter of choice! You can be as good or as bad as you want to be!

Moral laws and ethical laws are for the *good of man. We have no code of ethics dealing in how one should be bad or evil,* and we are all bound by ethical and moral law. Paul, in the Book of Romans, writes, "All who have sinned without the law will also perish without the law, and all who have sinned under the law will be judged by the law. For it is not the hearers of the law who are righteous before God, but the doers of the law who will be justified. When the Gentiles who have not the law do by nature what the law requires, they are a law to themselves, even though they do not have the law. They show that what the law requires is written on their hearts, while their conscience also bears witness, and their conflicting thoughts accuse or perhaps excuse them on that day when according to my gospel, God judges the secrets of men by Christ Jesus." What he is saying is that if one stands under the law he is bound by it, If he does not stand under the law, one is bound by his actions and not the law.

Paul also protests against the mechanical, meaningless type of conformity that many worshippers of God practice, through their rituals and not in their hearts. His position is that it is not the mere performance of an outward act, whether in worship or in one's attitude towards his fellow man, that constitutes obedience to God, but the conscious willingness to obey. Unless the individual convinces himself of the rightness of obedience, unless he possesses or achieves an unshakable faith, righteous does not truly represent his actions if he is aware of God and His laws, *but only if he is not aware of God and His laws*. The sinner who sincerely repents is more virtuous than one who merely conforms to doctrine through habit or ritual. The emphasis on faith is an emphasis on what is in one's heart. In Micah we read, "What doeth the Lord require of thee, only to do justly, and to love mercy, and to walk humbly with thy Lord." And Christ said, "Blessed are the poor in spirit, for theirs is the kingdom of heaven . . . blessed are the pure in heart for they shall see God."

Many of the letters printed in "Dear Abby" go like this: "My husband is a good man. He brings his paycheck home and is good to the kids. He doesn't stay out at night, pays his bills and is really a wonderful man. But, Abby, I have a problem; he never shows me any affection. It's just like all he does is because of his duty. It's like he feels that he is in a trap and can't get out of it and that what he does is because he has to. If he would just tell me that he loves me and would show me a little attention then I'd be happy too. I'd leave him if it wasn't for the kids because I need to know that he truly loves me and that is all I have ever asked of him. Signed, Lonely Heart."

This is what Paul is saying; if you do good works, do it because you are willing to do them, out of love, and not because it is a Christian duty, or out of fear, or out of a hope for a reward. Good works are not enough without a conscious willingness to serve God, simply because you love Him and not because you think you deserve reward for your works. You can't go out and do good works because you think that if you do God will reward you with the gift of righteousness, and expect to gain that gift. But, if you do good works simply because you want to do good works without thought of reward, then you have hope. To put it bluntly, you cannot pay money to the church, do good works, serve your fellow man out of duty, and then turn to God and say, "Look, God, at the good things I have done, now you owe me salvation." *Because God does not owe you one whit.* Good works not done willingly, out of love, but because of a desire for reward, or with the idea of earning salvation, has no reward. Salvation is not earned, it is a gift of love from God in return for your love for him as reflected by your inner attitude and not by your outer attitude or acts. Once you enter into a correct relationship, a relationship of love with God, you cannot do otherwise than do good works, out of gratitude for his love and saving grace, and not out of a hope for reward.

Almost all moral and ethical laws can be equated to what was, or is, in one's heart; men may think they know what is in another's heart, but only that person truly knows—and God.

Love cannot be fully explained or reasoned out, one either loves or he does not. We can explain things that are real in nature, but not values; electricity and matter, but not beauty and goodness. Man is the only animal that spends endless hours in the pursuit of beauty. Men landscape their homes, decorate the interior, spend hours on a painting or work of sculpture, and on and on, all of which contributes not one whit to his survival. The animal is content to find a dry cave for rest, safety, and to bear its young; all other endeavors are designed for survival and nothing more. An exception is possibly the dog, who will give up his normal love for his master out of love. These higher values of man, among which are moral and ethical laws, must be derived from a supreme source, one which invests our lives with significance and purpose and which enables us to evaluate good and evil, right and wrong, both from a practical, ethical standpoint of being members of a society, and from the moral standpoint of being obedient to God.

Why should we believe that obedience to moral and ethical laws is of any value outside of living with our breathren? There is an axiom which says, "If there is evidence favoring an opinion, we ought to believe it; if the evidence is contrary to it, we ought to disbelieve it; and if there is no evidence pro or con, we ought to remain in doubt." This fits doubt well, but is has no place in faith, for faith is a belief, *not because of evidence, but in the absence of evidence.* There are things of which we shall never have any absolute knowledge. They cannot be proved, but nevertheless it is justifiable to have faith in their existence. There is a story which substantiates this position:

Once there were two friends. One was a real rounder, always drinking, chasing after women and gambling, brawling and really living it up. His friend was a God-fearing man who lived the quiet life, content with his life and with God. One day his friend asked him, "John, what are you going to do when you die and find out there is no heaven, and you missed out on all the fun I am having? It'd be like throwing away your life, wouldn't it?'' And John replied, ''Oh, I don't know, at least I'd know I did what I thought best and lived up to my highest ideals; but, by the way, what are you going to do when you die and find out there is a Hell?''

In Galatians we read, ''Do not be deceived, God is not mocked, for whatever a man sows, that he will also reap. For he who sows to his own flesh will from the flesh reap corruption, but he who sows to the Spirit will from the Spirit reap eternal life, and let us not grow weary in well-doing, for in due season we shall reap if we do not lose heart.''

The ethics that Jesus taught in the Sermon on the Mount must not be watered down and explained away, for these teachings serve as a standard which we as Christians ought to follow, for they form a code of ethical and moral behavior which stands as a measure of our success or failure. The ultimate importance to us *is not Christ's teachings, but His reality*, for He became the standard for our lives by living by what He taught, and we are called to imitate Him with lives of devotion and trust. The life of Christ stands as a rebuke for our petty quibbling, our play with words and our constant search for less costly ways of serving God. How often, when we have justified doing a thing in our minds, do we pick a quarrel with another because of what he said? This causes us to examine our own conscience, and we challenge what was said in the hope that the basis of our own justification will not be destroyed. He who seeks to possess a worthy life at little cost and through justification needs to be reminded that Christ gave everything, even His life, in the service of God. We should not offer less than this, and in the least should offer to live lives in His service. God may not accept less than this. It is a source of amazement to me how often exception is taken to the Bible, or to a lesson, or during a discussion, to the mere use of a single word, or sentence, or idea, rather than trying to understand the underlying message that is being revealed. *We can nit-pick the Bible all day long, but not the messages, the doctrines, the laws of right and wrong, the moral laws, the ethical laws, the laws of love, of trust, of devotion, and of faith.* To use a modern term, the secret to understanding the Bible comes from reading ''between the lines'' to discover the underlying flow of revealed truths. The wisdom and knowledge we miss during our Biblical studies through nit-picking must form a source of humor for our Lord, and surely He has a sense of humor, or else He would hurry doomsday!

Without moral laws and ethical laws it would be impossible for men to have fellowship with God or with his fellow man, and, of course, the animal world does nicely without them, except in the case of hunting packs and group survival. But even here there are exceptions; for example, rocks are very hard to come by in the anarctic, and in the penguin roost if one penguin is caught stealing a rock from another's nest for his own use, he is set upon by others and severely beaten and sometimes driven out of the community.

Most of us have little problem accepting the basic teachings of our faith. We accept the fatherhood of God and the doctrine of brotherhood to man. We accept the idea of love of God and love of neighbor, but put it into practice and it becomes quite another matter, for we are all quite proficient in justifying what we do, even to the point, when necessary, of outright rejection of Biblical moral and ethical laws that are contrary to what we feel or believe, or want to do. We admit that we do wrong, but then say, "Yes, I did wrong, but . . . " then we justify what we do.

"Let your conscience be your guide" is a well-known saying, but this is not enough for the Christian, for conscience not in tune with the disciplines of God will not fulfill his responsibility as a Christian. The son of a headhunter can take the head of another, shrink it and hang it in his tepee, and his conscience will not bother him in the least. To think a thing, or to do a thing, and then justify it solely on conscience, is an impudence, if it is not weighed against the moral and ethical teaching of God. It is here that the point of departure must be established or else our conclusions are fradulent.

Some people believe that sincerity is the criterion. But the sincerity with which a person maintains a position or belief is no indication of its moral or ethical value. One may sincerely hate someone but that most assuredly violates moral laws. Some of the worst crimes in history were perpetrated by men and women whose sincerity cannot be doubted—witness the current killing between different religious factions in the Middle East and Ireland, the Spanish Inquisition and the Salem witch trials. Here, again, sincerity must be weighted against God's laws in order to have validity.

Self-justification is another mistaken guideline. Often we take the position that no one was hurt by what we did. Politicians have been heard to say that they took a payoff because the bids were identical and one bidder offered a kickback the others did not, and the public paid the same price anyway. Of course, the fact that the bid granted could have been reduced by the amount of the payoff does not enter into the considerations of anyone who seeks after self-justification. Expense accounts are padded because, well, the person wouldn't have spent the money if he hadn't been on the trip. When one receives more change than he is entitled to, he may say that the store could afford the loss better than he could do without, etc., etc. The danger of yielding to small moral breaches is that it increases the ability to justify larger acts.

The basis for morality in our religion is the will of God as revealed in His word, as expressed in the Ten Commandments, the Sermon on the Mount, the doctrine of brotherly love, and so forth. Christians are convinced that God is righteous, and find in Him the basis for moral order. The Bible and other world religions indicate that whenever the actions of men revealed a loss of faith in the righteous of God, that He brought forth great teachers and prophets to restore that faith. The prophet Amos appeared in Israel at a time when the idea of a just God was being openly questioned. Amos spent little time denouncing the moral sins of Israel, but concentrated on their ethical transgressions. His position was that one's attitude towards one's neighbor was an expression of their attitude towards God. When a man has moral values, then ethical values follow as a matter of course, or else one is not a moral man. *The ethical man is not necessarily the moral man, but a moral man cannot be unethical if he is truly moral!*

Paul told his listeners that if they found a man of low morals and ethics in their church they should throw him out and have nothing more to do with him. This, at first blush, does not appear to be ethically sound and appears to be extremely high-handed and not worthy of one who professes to be a Christian. However, one must realize that Paul was a man of love and what he was trying to convey is that if such a person is found among you and you accept him and overlook his evil ways and do not censor him, then you have no chance at all of saving his soul. But if you do censor him then he might come to his senses, and in that event, it may be possible that you might be able to save his soul. This is a position of love and it is therefore expedient that we do not act before all facts are available, but once available, that we do what we ought to do in order to save our friend from condemnation. This is not an act of judging, and then passing condemnation, it is an act of love. If we judge we condemn, if we love we do not condemn, but assist our struggling brothers even though the act taken may be difficult and may appear to be unchristianlike.

As to judging others, Paul also wrote in Romans:

"Therefore you have no excuse, O man, whoever you are when you judge another, for in passing judgment upon him you condemn yourself, because you, the judge, are doing the very same things. We know that the judgment of God rightly falls upon those who do such things. Do you suppose, O man, that when you judge those who do such things and yet do them yourselves, you will escape the judgment of God? Or do you presume upon the riches of His kindness and forbearance and patience? Do you not know that God's kindness is meant to lead you to repentance? But by your hard and impenitent heart you are stirring up wrath for yourself on the day when God's righteous judgement will be revealed. For he will render to every man according to his works, to those who by patience in well-doing seek for glory and honor and immortality, He will give eternal life, but those who are factious and do not obey the truth, but obey wickedness, there will be wrath and fury. There will be tribulation and distress for every human being who does evil, the Jew first and also the Greek, but glory and honor and peace for everyone who does good, the Jew first and also the Greek."

Thus the act of judging another is considered to be an act of immoral consequences—this right has been reserved by God.

Paul also continued in Romans:

"Now we know that whatever the law says it speaks to those who are under the law, so that every mouth may be stopped, and the whole world may be held accountable to God."

What Paul is saying is that all are under the law, all have broken the law and stand condemned under it, thus we need to accept Christ and if we do then we will be forgiven, even though we break the law. If one accepts Christ in his heart he cannot do otherwise than strive to obey the law. So, once more, the ethical man is not necessarily the moral man, but the truly moral man cannot be other than the ethical man.

We are all of this world and we, as men and women, must strive to be strong in will, must strive for immortality, strive to seek after knowledge of God, to find the truth, and then not yield to the pressures of evil. We must cherish that which is good and which we are fortunate enough to experience, but we must be strong enough to also bear evil which is all about us, and each day with stout hearts and conviction we must strive to reduce its influence. We all strive, in faith, towards one goal and we are caught up in the motion of life; some of us will go down, other will survive, but we must all pray and hope that before life ends someone, somewhere, will do a work of noble worthiness which will cause all men to seek to obey the moral and ethical laws of God.

IV

Temptation

The word "tempt" means to endeavor to persuade, to induce, entice. To lead, or endeavor to lead into evil. To entice to do what is wrong by promise of pleasure or gain. The word "temptation" means the act of tempting.

Perhaps the word temptation was improperly recorded or interpreted in that part of the Lord's Prayer which reads, "lead us not into temptation, but deliver us from evil." It is doubtful if Jesus, or anyone else, could believe that God would deliberately lead us into temptation, or try to entice us to do wrong or to commit evil. If the words are recorded correctly, then it indicates that they did think that He might, and therefore the plea that He not do so. It is difficult to believe that this was the intent, and it is possible that the pleading has been improperly interpreted.

In support thereof, James wrote as follows:

"Blessed is the man who endures trial, for when he has stood the test he will receive the crown of life which God has promised to those who love him. Let no one say when he is tempted, 'I am tempted by God'; for God cannot be tempted with evil and He himself tempts no one; but each person is tempted when he is lured and enticed by his own desire. Then desire, when it has conceived, gives birth to sin; and when it is fullgrown brings forth death."

You will recall the temptation of Christ by Satan which is recorded in Luke: "And Jesus, full of the Holy Spirit, returned from the Jordan, and was led by the Spirit for forty days in the wilderness, tempted by the Devil. And He ate nothing in those days; and when they ended He was hungry. The Devil said to him, 'If you are the Son of God, command this stone to become bread.' And Jesus answered him, it is written, 'Man shall not live by bread alone.' And the Devil took Him up, and showed Him all the kingdoms of the world in a moment of time and said to Him, 'To you I will give all this authority and their glory; for it has been delivered to me, and I will give to whom I will. If you, then, will worship me, it shall all be yours.' And Jesus answered him, it is written, 'You shall worship the Lord your God, and Him only shall you serve.'

"And he took Him to Jerusalem, and set Him on the pinnacle of the temple, and said to Him, 'If you are the Son of God, throw yourself down from here; for it is written, 'He will give angels charge of you, to guard you, and on their hands they will bear you up, lest you strike you foot against a stone.' And Jesus answered him, it is said, 'You shall not tempt the Lord your God.' ' "

Who was this man Christ, that He could resist such temptations? We know a great deal about ourselves, but what about Christ? We evaluate ourselves as being martyrs, geniuses or inferior beings, glamorous or ugly, successful or failing, but it is doubtful that we are capable of resisting all temptations that are put in our way. Even Paul, you will remember, lamented that he tried to do good, but that evil was always at hand tempting him. The better we understand Jesus the easier it is to understand our lives. In Him we see what we could and should be, and are not. Of course, we can excuse ourselves by saying that it was easy for Him, because He was the Son of God, while we are mere mortals. It is important to understand that Christ was not immune to moral conflicts, *and that the victory He achieved was a real, human victory, and if it was not, then His victory would be meaningless to us, and His promises null and void.*

If you were asked, "Who are you?" you would probably respond that you are a businessman, a lawyer, a housewife, a mother, etc. We all like to identify ourselves as being something besides a mere human being. When we meet people we are inclined to say, "I am Mr. Brown, I work for Company X"; or, "I am Doctor Smith"; and if nothing more, "I am John Jones, I live down the street." Well, who did Christ say He was? Let's search some of the Scriptures and read about who He said He was.

John wrote: "God is spirit, and they that worship Him must worship Him in spirit and in truth. The woman said to Him, 'I know that the Messiah is coming, who is called Christ; when He comes, He will show us all things." Jesus said to her, '*I who speak to you am He.*' John also wrote: "But Jesus answered them saying, my Father is working still, and I am working."

And there is this passage in John:

"You search the scriptures, because you think that in them you have eternal life; and it is the scriptures that bear witness to me; yet you refuse to come to me that you may have life. I have come in my Father's name, and you do not receive me.' Jesus said to them, 'I am the bread of life, he who comes to me shall not hunger, and he who believes in me shall never thirst. But I said to you that you have seen me and yet do not believe. All that the Father gives me will come to me; and him who comes to me I will not cast out. For I have come down from heaven not to do my own will, but the will of Him who sent me, that I should lose nothing of all that He has given me, but raise it up at the last day. *For this is the will of my Father, that everyone who sees the Son and believes in Him should have eternal life; and I will raise him up at the last day.* I am the living bread which came down from heaven, if anyone eats of this bread, he will live forever, and the bread which I shall give for the life of the world is my flesh. I shall be with you a little longer, and then I go to Him who sent me; you will seek me and you will not find me; where I am you cannot come. I am the light of the world, He who follows me will not walk in darkness, but will have the light of life. Even if I do bear witness to myself, my testimony is true, for I know whence I come and whither I am going, but you do not know whence I come or whither I am going. You judge according to flesh, I judge no one. Yet even if I do judge, my judgment is true, for it is not I alone that judge, but I and He who sent me. In your law it is written that the testimony of two men is true; I bear witness to myself, and the Father who sent me bears witness to me. You are from below, I am from above; you are of this world, I am not of this world, I told you that you would die in your sins, for you will die in your sins unless you believe that I am He. I am the resurrection and the life, he who believes in me, though he die, yet shall he live, and whosoever lives in me shall never die. Do you believe this? Let not your hearts be troubled, believe in God, believe also in me. In my Father's house are many mansions, if it were not so, would I have told you that I go to prepare a place for you? And when I go and prepare a place for you, I will come again and will take you to myself . . . I am the way, and the truth, and the life; no one comes to the Father, but by me. If you had known me, you would have known my Father also; henceforth you know Him and have seen Him. So you have sorrow now, but I will see you again and your hearts will rejoice, and no one will take your joy from you.''

Now, of course, each and every one of us has a perfect, free right to accept or to reject everything that Christ said of Himself. *But it is inconceivable that the human mind could have conceived such in-depth thoughts, or could give so much hope to struggling humanity.* In fact, it is difficult to imagine that a mere mortal would have so much compassion for the world that he would even try to conceive such thoughts for the benefit of other men, let alone actually do so. What He said in itself indicates that His words were divinely inspired and put forward to man through Christ. It is difficult to believe that there can be doubt as to the validity of His claims, and that He truly was the Son of God.

Thus, we have a man born of the flesh, in human form, who was tempted as we are, and even more through direct contact with Satan in the wilderness, who threw temptations and taunts at him: ''If you are the Son of God then do these things and then everyone will believe in you.'' These same challenges were hurled at Him as He hung upon the Cross. In Matthew we read: ''And those who passed by derided Him, wagging their heads and saying, 'You who would destroy the temple and build it in three days, save yourself! If you are the Son of God, come down from the cross.' So also the chief priests, with the scribes and elders, mocked Him, saying, 'He saved others, He cannot save Himself. He is the King of Israel; let Him come down now from the cross, and we will believe in Him. He trusts in God; let God deliver Him now, for He said, I am the Son of God. And the robbers who were crucified with Him also reviled HIm in the same way.''

Had He responded to these challenges and reacted as a mortal, it would have shown weakness, for He would be using the power of God for His own purposes and glory, *and not for the glory of God*. He would have responsed to vanity, and people would then say that He was tempting God and that He was a fake, because He feared death and did not Himself believe in eternal life. If he had picked up the gauntlet and come down from the cross He would have been, in effect, saying "All right, you doubters, behold what I do!" And then with flashes of lighting and thunder he could have come down, but then He would have denied His real humanity, including death and suffering. Had He yielded to the taunts and temptations to come down from the cross, He would have betrayed His mission; *to die for the sins of the world so that men might have life.*

The use of the word "temptation" in the Bible means much more than the everyday use of the word, such as in the case of our being tempted to overeat, or to break a diet by eating candy, etc., but when the Bible uses the word "tempt," it means that someone or some influence tempts a person to commit an immoral act, and that person, in turn, must then respond to the temptation, either by giving in to it and doing that which is against his principles, or by resisting it and holding fast to his principles.

Biblical temptation is a very serious matter, and involves a personal belief in the conflicting powers in the universe: one, the power of God to guide our behavior, and the other, the power of evil to divert us from our obedience to God. It is no simple matter for one to be torn between his love of God and his love of pleasure. To know true temptation is to enter into an inner conflict with one's self and results in inner quarrels, with self-justification and excuses always running in the foreground. Many times, when we do yield, afterwards we experience deep remorse and desire for forgiveness, and if the remorse is deep enough it can result in suicide and tragedy. So to yield to temptatin in a Biblical sense is not a thing to be taken lightly.

We have taken a look at the man Jesus and at who He says He is, and this should enable us to further evaluate the temptations that He experienced in the wilderness.

The temptations to turn the stone into bread is symbolic of our universal human tendency to yield to our appetites for pleasure and satisfaction. When Christ responded that "man does not live by bread alone," it meant that He would not yield to the temptations of the flesh, but would fulfill first the needs of the spirit. Denials of self-pleasures and evil always lead to spiritual strength and growth.

The temptations to rule over all the world's kingdoms is symbolic of human ambition, of our lust for power, and the fulfillment of personal ambitions for our own self-satisfaction. Men love such things when they yield to the flesh, but Jesus said that God alone is to be worshipped and served, that here is the true greatness of a man and leads to spiritual fulfillment.

The temptation to jump from the pinnacle of the temple in a display of open defiance of natural law is symbolic of native, human arrogance.

It would have resulted in tempting God to either save Him or let Him fall to His death. It would have been a display of conceit by showing that He was truly the Son of God, and therefore beyond the flesh. But Jesus said that you shall not tempt God.

Thus we have Jesus, conceived in the flesh, with all of the human frailties, resisting these temptatins, and they were not easy things to resist. His resistance is a testimony to His unfailing love and devotion for the Father.

Most of us are not tempted to turn stones into bread, to rule over kingdoms, or to perform death-defying stunts; we are, nevertheless, tempted each day to deny God and yield to temptations. It is by resisting these temptations that we grow in spirit, in a deeper love for God, and belief in His Son, Jesus. We all have certain secret desires to be able to do the things that Christ resisted. We Love to watch magic, and we like to do tricks that confound our friends. If we could turn stones into bread, we probably would do so, because it would make us the greatest of magicians in the eyes of our friends. We would love the praise that would come our way. We may not desire to rule kingdoms, but we all like to get ahead, to be the boss, or a vice-president or the president of a company, or be boss of the household, or be the captain of the team, or, at the least, the best in the field of endeavor that we are engaged in. *This is not wrong if it does not become the primary goal in our lives*, but only if it does, because one simply cannot love these things and love God also. If we worship power, money, position, leadership, etc., then we cannot love God with the fulness of our hearts.

John said: "Do not love the world or the things in the world. If any one loves the world, love for the Father is not in Him."

Then we all like to show off a little. We like to watch death-defying circus acts, race down the highway over the speed limit, take chances in the face of danger, tempting fate and God. But Jesus said, "You shall not tempt the Lord your God."

When we compare the things we do with what Christ refused to do, then the extent of His refusal becomes real and meaningful and serves as a guideline for our own thoughts and actions.

Whenever we resist temptation it has an uplifting effect upon our whole being. Many times on a Sunday morning we are tempted to remain in bed and not go to church, but we force ourselves to rise, get dressed, and attend church, somewhat against our will. But later we feel better for having done so, and, in most cases, are glad that we did. We feel a sense of victory.

Whenever someone hurts us, or offends us, we are tempted to strike back, to get even. But when we resist the impulse it make us feel good, we feel stronger and happier. This can, of course, in and of itself, become an evil, when we glory in our own good works and we may not give the credit to Christ who taught us how we should live with our fellow man. Self-respect is a healthy state, for if we downgrade ourselves others will surely follow.

Egoism, however, is excessive love and thought of one's self, and in ethics it means that self-interest is the valid end of all action, or the motive of all conscious action. Egotism means constant referral to one's self or excessive use of the word "I." The best guideline to use when we are successful in resisting temptation is to pause for a moment and say, "Thank you for giving me the strength, the courage, and the know-how to resist the temptation with which I was confronted."

If one were to attempt to list all the temptations which confront us all of our lives, it would take many, many volumes of print. Nevertheless, it is pleasant to pause and look back over our lives and recall to memory how many of them we did resist, and they constitute victory over temptation. What we did, in effect, was to say, "Get thee behind me Satan," and the more often we say it, the stronger we become, the more character we develop, and the more worthy are our lives.

The problem of looking back is that we likewise recall to memory the many times that we did not resist temptation, but yielded to it, and this makes us feel uncomfortable because it is difficult to indulge in self-criticism and self-evaluation. Then, many times there remains some doubt in our minds whether we have really been forgiven for our shortcomings in the face of temptation, and we worry about it. If we are honest with ourselves we all have "skeletons in our closets."

God's promise to us, given through Christ, is that He gave His Son's life to us so that we might have forgiveness of sin and that, "whosoever believes in Him (the Son), though he die, yet shall he live, and whosoever lives in Him shall never die," and it is this assurance that causes us to strive to achieve victory over temptation, and this knowledge causes our soul to soar to new heights on the "wings of eagles."

V

Evil

Any presentation dealing with evil is most difficult, for one of the first questions is, "Why does evil exist in the world?" and the answer, "Because Adam ate an apple" does not suffice. There have been thousands of pages written on this subject, conjecture, speculation, and moralizing, but none produce any satisfactory answers.

There are many misconceptions regarding the meaning and result of evil, such as sometimes evil begets good, and good begets evil. First, almost all good, materially speaking, results in some evil to someone else: one gains, one loses. Misguided good often produced an overbalance of evil, and an act thought to be good will often produce an evil greater than the evil one seeks to rectify. For example, the Germans believed in individual freedom so strongly that to prohibit the existence of the Nazi Party would be evil, for both sides would not be heard, and its prohibition would inhibit freedom and might set a precedent which would restrict other freedoms. So, yielding to the moralists, the Nazi Party came into being, and we all know the result. *Today we find the same philosophy gaining astounding acceptance in this nation, both politically, legally, and otherwise.*

Both good and evil have a natural tendency to produce more of its own kind, not the opposite. The ordinary and predominant tendency of good is towards more good. Health, strength, wealth, knowledge, virtues, are not only good in themselves but facilitate and promote the acquisition of good, both of the same and of other kinds. The person who can learn easily is one who already knows much; it is the strong and not the sickly person who can do everything that is most conducive to health; those who find it easy to gain money are not the poor but the rich. Health, strength, knowledge, and talents are all means of achieving success and happiness, and success is often the indispensable means of acquiring the good things in life which makes one happy, yet many hold that success is immoral.

Whatever may be said about evil turning into good, the general tendency of evil is towards further evil. Bodily illness renders the body more susceptible to disease, and sometimes produces physical defects so great that exertion is impossible and disability of the mind so great that the person cannot do any productive thing to maintain subsistence. All severe pain, either physical or mental, tends to increase the susceptibility for pain and torment. Poverty produces a thousand mental and moral evils. When one is hurt or oppressed it lowers the whole tone of life. One bad action usually leads to more bad actions, both upon the doer and by others involved. Almost all material gains are arrived at the expense of certain moral beiefs, and those who are successful are usually branded as being immoral because they will not share what they have with the have-nots. That some evils become good and some good becomes evil cannot be denied, but the majority of good and evil beget like kinds.

Likewise, we often say that a person's character is formed for him and not by him. That it results from his parentage and society and the environment to which he was born and so, therefore, he has no power to alter it and should not be held accountable for his acts. *But this is an error, for every man has, to a certain extent, the power to alter his character.* We may say that a man's character is formed for him, but nothing was done to take away his desire to remold it. He may not have control over the conditions of his birth, but he does have control over the remodeling of the character which he inherited, discounting disease, heredity, and genes, over which man exercises no control. If society caused one to be born under certain circumstances, then it imposes its will upon the individual; but likewise the individual can, if he truly desired to do so, place himself under different circumstances *if he will but put forth the effort.* All of us are as capable of making our own character, if we will it, as others are for making it for us. We are not speaking of material benefits, but character, which is quite apart from materialism. Many poor people become noble in character, and many successful men seem to have none at all. So things that we call evil do not necessarily produce persons low in character, nor affluence produce those noble in character. Aside from mental or physical deformities, if one has the will, he can alter and remold his character. If our point of reference is, however, materialism, then you have quite a different picture. But we are speaking of good and evil, neither of which are dispensed out differently to the rich or to the poor, for involvement therein appears to be equal in both.

We are all caught up in the conflict between good and evil, all of us, the rich and the poor, the meek and the strong, the pagan and the worshippper—all are caught up. You will recall Paul's lament:

"So I find it to be a law that when I want to do right, evil lies close at hand. For I delight in the law of God, in my inmost self, but I see in my members another law at war with the law of my mind and making me captive to the law of sin which dwells in my members. Wretched man that I am! Who will deliver me from this body of death? Thanks be to God through Jesus Christ our Lord. So then, I of myself serve the law of sin. There is therefore now no condemnation for those who are in Jesus Christ. For the law of the spirit of life in Jesus Christ has set me free from the law of sin and death. For God has done what the law, weakened by the flesh, could not do, sending His own Son in the likeness of sinful flesh and for sin, he condemned sin in the flesh.''

Sin enters into the world from outside of God's creation and it enters into man when it is not opposed, or yielded to it. Each man dies his own death because each man commits his own sins and to sin is to die. Paul holds every man to be personally responsible and accountable for his own sins and death. But Christ offers man an alternative to death and that is acquittal from the law of sin and death through belief in Him. No man is so guilty under the law, so depraved, or so degraded as to be beyond that point where God will not forgive him, if he repents and accepts Chrsit as the one who will intervene for him and gain him acquittal before God.

Well, who will gain acquittal? It is those whose actions correspond to the will of God, and contrary thereto, those whose actions do not correspond to the will of God will not be acquitted. The Jew believes that acquittal will be gained by obeying the law, but Paul teaches that it cannot be earned, for all fall short of the law, but could be received only as a gift from God through our faith in Christ. Paul teaches acquittal by faith and not by works.

Paul flatly denies that the Christian has earned anything before God by his righteousness, although he does not deny that righteousness has an ethical aspect. What he does deny is that ethical righteousness merits the believer one whit before God. In other words, what Paul is saying is that *righteousness is not a possession that one has earned, but it is the verdict that God pronounced concerning him. The decisive factor in a man's life is the verdict under which he stands, quite aside from his performance.* He is pronounced either as "acquitted" or "guilty." What God regards one to be is what one is and not what one thinks oneself to be, or what another thinks one to be. It is only when God regards one to be a sinner that one is a sinner. If, therefore, God declares one to be righteous, one is righteous, and this is not the result of his works or his self-evaluations. Salvation becomes a possibility only in the relationship of man to God and not on his performance, for it is axiomatic that one who has a correct relationship with God cannot do otherwise but perform in accordance with the will of God.

For Paul, an act done in faith is not sinful, for an act done in faith is not done for reward but is done in gratitude—gratitude to God for the life He has offered in Jesus Christ.

This is why Paul warns agianst boasting. By boasting he does not mean verbal bragging, but he means the inner attitude that assumes that one merits something from God for his good works. It is precisely because any ethical behavior that grows out of obedience to the law gives ground for boasting that it is always a sin. Paul makes a distinction between the compulsion of law and the compulsion of love. If one keeps the law rather than breaks it, he merits a reward under the law and deserves to be recognized as different from those who break the law. But if one does a deed because love compels it, *he does not merit anything,* and if the one upon whose behalf one acted through love is offered a reward, it would be offensive, for then you would know that the act was not interpreted as truly an act of love. It is not the character of love to seek after reward. All love ever requires is love.

The Christian is not righteous because he acted in obedience to the law, but rather because he has acted in love, out of gratitude for acquittal. It is not what a believer has done that makes him righteous in the ethical sense, but why he has done it. But the ethical man cannot do other than strive to do good, for it follows as the day does the night.

It is important that one realizes that he *will not be judged by what he knows, but by what he does,* and unless one can judge himself innocent, then he is guilty of the things he judges his brothers to be guilty of, and this is self-condemning. God judges the thoughts of men, not their knowledge, nor their acts. It is important to realize that if one rejects Christ, then he is judged under the law for his works and is not judged because of his faith in the atonement of Christ. One may either appear in faith in Jesus Christ and accept reconciliation through Christ, or one may appear outside of faith, rejecting God's gift and pointing instead to one's performance. But herein lies the danger, for one who appeals for acquittal under the law must rest his case exclusively upon his performance, and one must be judged by his performance in relation to all the law and not simply in relation to the laws he managed to keep.

One's relationship to law is that one is guilty if one is found to have broken any one of the laws. When a man is arrested and taken before a judge he is not asked how many laws he has kept, but which one he has broken, and if he breaks a single law, he is guilty. Who among us can state that he has never broken a single one of God's laws, and thereby is entitled to acquittal under the law? Even though you do good works all the livelong day, if you break the law you are condemned under that law, and if you don't believe me, let me see you break one of man's laws and rob a store and see how quickly you are sent to prison even though you obeyed all of the other laws of the land, and did good works all day long. Under God's laws, who would gain acquittal? Acquittal is not possible under God's laws, for all fall short of it, but nevertheless *acquittal is offered apart from and around the law through Jesus Christ.* He makes acquittal available to everyone who will take it. It is a free gift. It is given for nothing but given as a gift of love and all love rquires is love. This is why Christ came and gave His life upon the Cross that whosoever liveth and believeth in Him shall not die but have everlasting life. Man is too weak to obey all of the law. God, in His mercy for man, who struggles so hard to obey and yet cannot, gave him a way apart from the law. *He gave the gift of life through the life of His Son, Jesus Christ.* It was a sacrifice. In the old days when men offered animals up to God on the altar, it was *not the body* of the animal that they were offering up *but the life* of the animal that was being sacrificed to God. When Christ died upon the Cross, it was His *life* that God sacrificed for man. All one needs to do is believe this, be grateful for the acquittal, love God for His sacrifice, and he is free from the laws of sin and death. It is up to each individual to decide if he seeks acquittal by good works under the law and obedience to the law, or acquittal through the love of Christ by having faith in Him, then do good works as a result of that love and belief with a willing heart, because we cannot do otherwise. It should not be a difficult choice, but it is for many.

But if you do so, do not be deceived into believing that now all will be milk and honey, for it will not be so. We are of the world, not apart from it, and as Paul said, "We rejoice in our suffering knowing that suffering produces endurance, and endurance produces character, and character produces hope, and hope does not disappoint us because God's love has been poured into our hears through the Holy Spirit which has been given to us."

A lot of people have left God and the church because they felt that neither did enough for them. They see death, sickness, wars, poverty, and on and on, either for themselves or for others, and they become disillusioned because they say, "I loved God, I prayed to Him, but things go on just the same. Why waste my time. I don't believe in it anymore." It is not this life that will reflect the love of God, but the afterlife. We are living in the world, of the world, and who wants to be babied and sheltered from all of life? It would avail nothing but self-satisfaction.

Paul sums it up like this:

"Therefore, since we are justified by faith, we have peace with God through our Lord Jesus Christ. Through Him we have obtained access to this grace in which we stand, and we rejoice in our hope of sharing the glory of God. While we were yet helpless, at the right time Christ died for us. Since, therefore, we are now justified by His blood, much more shall we be saved by Him from the wrath of God. For if while we were enemies we were reconciled to God by the death of His Son, much more, now that we are reconciled, shall we be saved by His life. Not only so, but we also rejoice in God through our Lord Jesus Christ, through whom we have now received our reconciliation."

"What is the origin of evil?" "What caused Satan to rebel against God?" These are age-old questions for which no completely satisfactory answer can be given. To ponder the questions with the expectation of an answer is as much of a waste of time as to ask the question, "Where did God come from?" We say that there should be no evil, that all things should be good, but this is only an assumption, for we do not know if things should be different or not, or even if they can be different. We know that things are as they are, or as they appear to be. Should discussions of good and evil be limited strictly to morality and ethical behavior and to man's relationship with his fellow man, or must we also include a discussion of nature? If we say yes, upon what authority do we arrive at this conclusion? We do not know if nature ought to be included in such considerations or not, for its inclusion might, of itself, be an evil thing that is injected into one's evaluation of good and evil for the sole purpose of confounding men's minds. *When one includes nature he is, whether he admits it or not, judging God*, and before a thing can be judged there must be a point of reference. Since nature cannot be our point of reference, there can be no good or evil in nature, for nothing in nature happens because the victim received his just desserts. No one can say that what happens to an animal is due to his conduct and that he got what he deserved, and without desserts, reward and punishment, how can there be evil?

All good and evil, moral and ethical behavior boils down to man's relationship with his fellow man and man's relationship with God, and nature does not enter into it at all. We are not wise enough to even say that things that happen in nature and which are hurtful to man are themselves evil, for we, being human, insist upon such evaluation in relationship to the events which occur in the universe, and not exclusively in relationship of man to God and man to man. That there are things in nature that appear to be evil cannot be denied, but then, neither can we confirm it, for things are not always as they appear to be, and they most assuredly are not as we always think they ought to be.

VI

Good and Evil

Just where does one draw the line between what is good and what is evil? For a thing to be good or evil it must have two elements: 1) the act committed must be voluntary; and 2) it must have a direct effect upon ourselves and upon our fellow man.

That whatever is done must be voluntary is not difficult to see, for if involuntary, it has no substance whatsoever. That it must have an effect upon ourselves or our fellow man, likewise, is not difficult to understand, for whatever we do either hurts or helps ourselves, mental or otherwise, or hurts or helps our fellow man, mental or otherwise, or else it is a futile act and is neither good nor evil.

One must have had a purpose or intended to achieve some personal gain or benefit, or intended to help or damage his fellow man before any act can be judged as good or evil. Whatever he does must either be for or at the expense of his fellow man, or in agreement with or contrary to his religious teachings, or in agreement with or contrary to the "norms" of the society of which he is a part, or else his acts cannot be judged good or evil.

In making the determination of good and evil, it is important to be very careful about judging another's acts, for first it must be determined whether the person being judged selected his act as a means of attaining personal benefit, or that circumstances justified the act. One should never judge another's acts by themselves, but should determine: 1) whether a choice was open to the person involved, and 2) the end purpose of the act taken. For example, if a man down on his luck, after pursuing all avenues open to him, finds no relief and steals food for his starving children, and those from whom he stole are no less wanting, is he to be judged as having committed a good act or an evil act? We say that it is evil to steal, *but is it any less evil to permit little children to starve to death?* Particularly when those from whom it was stolen suffered no great damage and refused to lift a finger to assist? Who in this example committed an act of evil and who an act of good? The man who stole or the persons who gave no help? Which would you judge? Do you see the problem with absolutes?

As Christians, our definitions of good and evil rest upon the ethical traditions of our religion because we take the position that all law rests in and is vested in God. Our position is that to transgress God's law is evil, and that to abide by it is good. *Our point of reference is not man's laws but God's laws.* Nevertheless, it should be remembered that we are extolled to be compassionate and understanding, and we are cautioned, "Judge not, lest ye be judged," for we do not know what is in the hearts of men, their motives, nor their mental agonies, while God does; thus, it is He who will judge the world, not us.

Many Christians do not willingly do acts of good or acts of evil, but do so simply because of their beliefs in reward and punishment. But here one must be careful, for reward does not function as an end result of good, but functions as an end in itself. Reward is gained when one does good deeds purely because he wants to abide by God's divine laws, out of his love for God, and not out of hope for a reward for his goodness, or out of fear of punishment if he is evil. If anyone does good deeds out of anticipation of reward, he fools himself. It is the free desire to abide by God's word that is of all importance. No matter what one does, it is the inner attitude that is controlling—what was the purpose of our acts: was it a free choice done because it is what we wanted to do or was it done under duress? *In other words, are we reluctant Christians or do we do that we do out of the sheer joy of serving God?*?

But how do we know what we do is good or evil? For one thing, there is in each of us a still, small voice which makes us feel guilty and unhappy before, during, and after wrongdoing. It is this that makes it possible to distinguish between good and evil and, to some extent, controls our conduct and many times makes us take a more difficult course in life. But where can we find guidelines that can cause us to come to the conclusion that this or that is absolutely good or absolutely evil? Well, that should be easy. Let us go to our ministers, our priests, and our theologians, becuase everyone knows that they are trained in the nature of God's character and are well-versed in His laws.

But the problem is that although they have knowledge of God's laws they do, from time to time, confess that they know not the true nature of God and admit there are many things about Him that are totally incomprehensible. The difficulty is that these ministers disagree among themselves regarding the true meaning of the laws of God, for they interpret them differently in each land, from each pulpit, for each denomination, for each religion, in each synagogue, temple, church, and before each altar. They each hold that truth has been revealed unto them and that all others are imposters and false teachers. They do admit that there is confusion in the interpretations of God's laws and they cannot agree among themselves concerning the nature of God's laws and are in perpetual dispute over who God has truly revealed truth! When one seeks their counsel he finds confusion, for they say they teach the one true religion, and all others are false teachers, yet each makes the same charge about the other.

How shall we know who speaks the truth and who speaks falsely? Each say, "We are correct and they are wrong." And, they back up their arguments by quoting from the word of God, but each quotes differently, *even though they quote from the same book!* And when from different books, they say, "My book is true, your book is false." Who speaks with the forked tongue and who with the two-edge sword? We cannot find absolutes there, so let us leave the conflicting doctrine of men and turn to the church herself!

But almost at once we run into theological disputes and into conflicting dogma! Each declares that they hold the keys to true knowledge and truth, some even say they hold the keys to heaven and hell. They are engaged in constant, petty quarreling and in past history have resorted to slaying one another, as in the case of the Crusades, and more recently, in Ireland and in the Middle East. They have committed heinous crimes against each other in the name of religion! Their members become enraged whenever any dogma is advanced contrary to what they believe to be "sound church doctrine." They advance a doctrine of love and peace, yet they war among themselves and in past history their members have resorted to savagery whenever their leaders extolled them to kill their enemies. A study of world churches throughout history reveals that no crime has ever been committed by man that has not also been done under the disguise of church doctrine, *under the dogma that what they do is pleasing to God*, yet both sides appeal to God for His help in obtaining victory over their enemies. But them, this is history. We now live in an intelligent, enlightened world and know that we are now on the one and only true path and because we are intellectuals we know that we follow the one and only true religion; *but have not all men, of all faiths, at all times, always said so?* No, there are no absolutes in church dogma so let us turn to nature—for are we not extolled by many that we should return to nature and that once having done so will find sublime happiness?

But at once we run into conflict, for what nature does does not always agree with our concept of good and evil. We look upon the act of killing as one of the greatest evils committed by man. Yet nature kills all the day long! She will, at one time or another, kill everything that lives, every blade of grass, every tree, every plant, every insect, all the fishes in the sea and the birds in the air, every animal, every man, woman and child, none shall escape her and many will die in agony and only after protracted tortures and suffering incomprehensible to man! Her cruelties are unbelievable, for she hurls giant storms and causes huge earthquakes to destroy the works of men and their lives. She causes men to be devoured by beast, she burns them to death with fire and flows of molten lava, she crushes them beneath rocks, smothers them in mudslides, drowns them in floods, starves them with hunger, freezes them to death, deprives them of life-giving water, poisons them with snake venom and with poisonous insects, cripples their minds and bodies, places poisonous plants and berries in their paths and entices them to eat thereof and die in agony. She strikes them down with bolts of lightning, impales them upon stakes, pins them beneath fallen trees, *and is completely indifferent to their cries of agony.* Some of her acts are more monstrous than anything man has ever conceived to do, and her violence never subsides in the animal, plant, insect, and water worlds, and she holds in reserve tortures not yet conceived in the minds of men. Everything done by man and called evil is done in nature—without compassion. Her conflict with our concept of good and evil is so great that we must quickly abandon her as a source of absolutes regarding good and evil and press on to the philosophers.

But here, immediately we run into conflict and trouble, for we learn that the basic purpose of philosophy is to attack man's religious and moral beliefs. Their logic is hard to refute, for in their writings they challenge the omnipotence and benevolence of God and proceed, step by step, to apply logic in support of their positions. They write book after book but they never agree among themselves upon any given conclusion. There is, however, some good in their writings which we can use in our search for the meaning of good and evil, for they qualify their logic and write:

"Men say that there ought not be evil, that is seems that things ought to be different, but this is assumption, for we do not know if things ought to be different or not, or for that matter, even if it could be different, or should be different. The only fact is, that it is not different, or it does not appear to be different. For things are as they are, or as they appear to be, and that should be self-evident and self-sufficient for any man of religion."

So we must abandon the philosophers in our search for absolutes and look elsewhere. But where? *Well, what in heaven's name is wrong with the word of God?* There can be no greater authority. Study the Scriptures, learn what He said, what He said through His Son Jesus Christ and His servants. We know the Ten Commandments, the golden rule, and doctrine of brotherly love, the Sermon on the Mount. They are doctrines of good and evil; they have withstood the test of time, no fault has been found in them, for these great doctrines are true and if anyone shall challenge the validity of your claim that they are true and from God, then tell them what Christ said: "Do not give dogs what is holy, and do not throw your pearls before swine, least they trample them underfoot and turn to attact you."

We should not make judgments of absolutes concerning what is good and what is evil, for we have neither the wisdom nor the knowledge to judge, but we do know in our own hearts what is good and what is evil. You have different feelings when you do good and when you do evil. We can fool every man but you cannot fool yourself!

Christ said, "Are you still without understanding? Do you not see that whatever goes into the mouth passes into the stomach, and so passes on?

But what comes out of the heart comes evil thoughts, murder, adultery, fornication, theft, false witness, slander. These are what defile a man.

"You shall love the Lord your God with all your heart, and with all your soul, and with all your mind. This is the great and first commandment. And a second like it, you shall love your neighbor as yourself. On these two commandments depend all the law and the prophets."

If you would truly know good and evil, read the Sermon on the Mount, review the Ten Commandments, read the doctrine of brotherly love, learn of love of man, love of God—it's at your fingertips, it's under our very noses. Beware of your judgments, for Christ said, "Judge not, that you be not judged. For with the judgment you pronounce you will be judged, and the measure you give will be the measure you get. Why do you see the speck that is in your brother's eye? Or how can you say to your brother, 'Let me take the speck out of your eye' when there is a log in your own eye. You hypocrite, first take the log out of your own eye, and then you will see clearly to take the speck out of your brother's eye."

It may surprise some of you to know that the Ten Commandments are 3,250 years old! They came into being around 1280 B.C. and have, as a guide to moral and ethical behavior, *remained unchanged since that time*. When you consider how many ethical codes have been written by man during this same period of time and proved to be inadequate and subsequently abandoned, it makes this record all the more astounding! Nations have come into being only to fade away to be replaced by other nations which themselves vanished. Great leaders, kings, czars, rulers have arisen, only to fall back into dust, but God's laws remain faithful and true. No ethinic code has ever been designed or conceived by the minds of men that has endured the test of time as have God's laws.

Omar Khayam wrote:

> "The wordly hope men set their hearts upon turn ashes—
> or it prospers, and anon,
> Like snow upon the Desert's dusty face,
> Lighting a little hour or two—is gone."

And so it is with the doctrines of men.
An anonymous wrote the following:

> "Isn't it strange that Princes and Kings,
> and Clowns that caper in sawdust rings,
> And ordinary folk like you and me
> are builders of Eternity?
>
> To each is given a book of rules,
> An hour glass, and a bag of tools,
> And each must build, ere his time has flown,
> A stumbling block—or a steppingstone."

Whenever one attempts to modify or change God's laws, they become a stumbling block—teach and abide by them and they become steppingstones.

So we may search out the wise old sages of the world, study their teachings, but in the end we always return to the only true doctrine of good and evil, the words given us by God through the Scriptures. John wrote the following:

"And now I beg you, not as though I were writing you a new commandment, but the one we have had from the beginning, that we love one another, and through this love we walk in His commandments, and this is the commandment, as you have heard from the beginning, that you follow love. Look to yourselves, that you may not lose what you have worked for, but may win full reward. Anyone who goes ahead and does not abide in the doctrine of Christ does not have God, but he who abides in the doctrines of Christ has both the Father and the Son. If anyone comes to you and does not bring this doctrine, do not receive him into the house or give him any greeting, for he who greets him shares his wicked world."

Can it be stated any plainer than that?

Need we look elsewhere for the meaning of good and evil than in the Holy Scriptures? How do we know our Scriptures are true? Faith!

VII

The Church

What is a church? Is it being a Methodist, a Baptist, a Presbyterian, or any other organized church? *It is not*, for these are merely denominations. Webster defines denominations as "a class, or society of individuals, called by the same name, a "sect," and defines "sect" as "one of the organized bodies of Christians." This definition probably should not limit itself to "Christians."

These various denominations usually develop from controversy through different interpretations of Scripture, and this has a certain tragic aspect because a house divided against itself cannot stand. Through division evil can divide and conquer; nevertheless, it also has certain advantages because when one looks back upon history when only one church was recognized, one finds a despotic church, a church that ruled with dictatorial power and who did not stop at torture and murder to maintain its infallibility and power. *Scripture was never intended to be an arena for argument, but was intended as a pathway to God.* But men choose to use Scripture as a basis for argument, as a basis for saying, "We are correct, you are wrong." When the extremists insist upon such a position, then the walls of the true church are weakened and the true meaning of the church becomes obscured and, indeed, sometimes denied.

The Hindus have a saying, "Divers are the way to ascend to the top of a house; one may use a rope, another the stairs, another a ladder, but all ascend to the top of the house." In other words, religious tolerance, not religious intolerance, which in and of itself is destructive of faith, for if carried too far it can lead to hate, not brotherly love; to conceit, not humbleness; and to might and not right.

What, then, is the church, the true church? Basically, the true church is comprised of persons who are members of the household of God. It is comprised of persons who have been joined together into a holy temple of the Lord, and are persons who are built into for it for a dwelling place of God in the Spirit. *For the Christian*, membership into the household of God is obtained through Jesus Christ, through faith in Him. All barriers are swept away, and man is both justified and made a member of the church by faith alone.

In Genesis we read that man was created in God's own image and there was brotherhood between man and God, in God's world. But man drifts away from the household of God and alienates himself and returns again into the household only when he returns to God of his own free will. Ephesians read, "Put off your old nature which belongs to your former manner of life of your mind, and put on the new nature, created after the likeness of God in true righteousness and holiness."

When men confess Christ and place their trust in Him then, as expressed in Ephesians, "So then you are no longer strangers and sojourners, but you are fellow citizens with the saints and members of the household of God, built upon the foundation of the Apostles and prophets, Christ Jesus Himself being the chief cornerstone, in whom the whole structure is joined together and grows into a holy temple in the Lord; in whom you also are built into it for a dwelling place of God in the Spirit."

In Matthew we read, "Now, when Jesus came into the district of Caesar's Philippi, He asked His disciples, 'Who do men say that the son of man is?' and they said, 'Some say John the Baptist, others say Elijah, and others Jeremiah or one of the prophets.' He said to them, 'But who do you say that I am?' Simon Peter replied, 'You are the Christ, the Son of the Living God.' And Jesus answered him, 'Blessed are you Simon Barjona! For flesh and blood have not revealed this to you, but my Father who is in heaven. And I tell you, you are Peter, and on this rock I will build my church, and the powers of death shall not prevail against it. I will give you the keys of the kingdom of heaven, and whatsoever you bind on earth shall be bound in heaven, and whatever you loose on earth shall be loosed in heaven.' "

The confession of Jesus as the Christ by anyone forms the foundation of the church for Him and we who confess Him are the building stones which form a part of the whole temple. But we, like Peter, are sometimes dismayed to find that our faith vanishes with hard times, yet when this confession is ours, we can build upon it. We must always be aware of the fact that the church is built upon weak men, men who confess their weakness, and acknowledge Christ, and when they do so they discover the power that is beyond their own. As Jesus said, "Even the power of death cannot prevail against such faith!"

The cornerstone, which is Christ, did not form the entire foundation— the prophets and apostles were included. The prophets of the Old Testament were men like Isaiah, who spoke God's word to men. The apostles were those who first witnessed the resurrection of Christ. The whole structure is joined together in Christ. He is the mortar that holds the faithful together. Though men may form denominations, sects, and groups, it is Christ who forms the bond that overcomes these differences if they truly believe in Christ and confess Him before men. As expresseed in I Corinthians, "For no other foundation can anyone lay than that which is laid, which is Jesus Christ. Do you not know that you are God's temple and that God's Spirit dwells in you? If anyone destroys God's temple, God will destroy him. For God's temple is holy, *and that temple you are.*"

We often think ourselves wise, that we do not need the Scriptures, that we can form our own religion, that we are too intellectual to go along with Scripture, that we can follow after the so-called arts of witchcraft, ESP, mysticism, fortune telling, dream interpretations, and any of the many and varied variations of beliefs. Putting forward first the new doctrine, and second, Christ as the foundation, but we ought to stop and read I Corinthians: "Let no one deceive himself; if any one among you thinks that he is wise in this age, let him become a fool that he may become wise. For the wisdom of this world is folly with God. For it is written, 'He catches the wise in their craftiness,' and again, 'The Lord knows that the thoughts of the wise are futile. So let no one boast of men, for all things are yours, whether Paul or Apollos of Cephas or the world or life or death or the present or the future, all are yours, and you are Christ's, and Christ is God's.' "

What this says to me is that when one has Christ he has the whole world and is the possessor of a wisdom that is beyond any doctrine that can be put forward by any man. *So why dilute that Wisdom, listening to the rantings of men*? If you are made a building block of the temple of God, what else is there to seek? Can it be that, perchance, we vacillate and waver in mind, and will, and convictions? It should not be so, for once you are set into the temple wall, and the mortar hardens, nothing can pry you loose from that binding force.

The early Christians were fully aware of soothsayers, fortune tellers, false doctrines, false religions, false gods, pagan rituals, and on and on, but when they accepted Christ they left all these things and clung to Christ. Many Christians today would reverse the trend. These early Christians were convinced that they were sons and daughters of God and as such, heir to His promises. They suffered the hostility of both Jews and Romans. They were competing with dozens of other religious sects. They were declared an illegal religion. Under these circumstances they could hardly have survived without a strong basis for courage. They found it in the confidence that God was with them in a special way, and that he had sacrificed His Son to tell them so. They were truly building blocks set into the church so firmly that nothing could pry them loose, not even torture and death! Do we possess such faith?

We of the church today continue to need the resources of the Scriptures. The early church lived by the Old Testament. Later, when the church came under persecution, they lived by the words of the evangelists through gospels and letters. Today we have both available to us, and they are unparalleled sources of wisdom to guide us along the way. *Controversies over the infallibility of the Bible need not concern us, nor should they prove to be an impairment to those who are true believers.* Any argument used by those who oppose biblical doctrine cannot be stated by them in absolutes, nor can they prove or disprove any part of it. We need not concern ourselves about it at all, for the great doctrine of salvation through Christ is the underlying message of the Bible, though the details may vary. The church will find its way through the Scriptures only, and only if, the Scriptures lead the church to God.

The church continues to need the ethical insights of both the Old and New Testaments. In these times when ethics are often developed from statistical data, when our morality is being examined by the so-called authorities and the wise men of our age, the church needs its foundation in the law of God to bring its members to a renewed obedience and acceptance of the will of God. It is not enough to be a member of an organization, but we must also be responsive to the purposes of God, and to human life expressed in the promises of God through His laws of life and love.

The Christian need not fear the assaults of the world or the turmoil within the church's institutions; these are neither new nor threatening if viewed within the centuries-old context of God's concerns for the spreading of His word among His people. The world may change, and we may change, but the word of God has remained constant and will so remain, no matter what the future holds for our denominations and our ministry. We will face trying times in the years to come, but if we accept Christ then we will stand steadfast in the face of the onslaughts of life in the simple, uncomplicated belief that Christ died for us that we may have life.

As Isaiah expressed it, "I am laying in Zion for a foundation a stone, a tested stone, a precious cornerstone, of a sure foundation." Isaiah said, "of a sure foundation", and if we believe that Christ does form a sure foundation for the church, then we need never fear His saying to us, as He did to the disciples when they were on the water in the storm, and cried out to Him that He save them, "Why are you afraid, O men of little faith?" But we can hope to hear the words, "Take heart, it is I, have no fear."

The description of Christ as the church is best described in Revelation. "Then I turned to see the voice that was speaking to me, and on turning I saw seven golden lampstands, and in the midst of the lampstands one like a son of man, clothed with a long robe and with a golden girdle around his breast; his head and his hair were white as white wool, white as snow; his eyes were like a flame of fire, his feet were like burnished bronze, refined as in a furnace, and his voice was like the sound of many waters; in his right hand he held seven stars, from his mouth issued a sharp two-edged sword, and his face was like the sun shining in full strength.

"And when I saw him, I fell at his feet as though dead, but he laid his right hand upon me, saying, "Fear not, I am the first and the last, and the living one, I died, an behold I am alive for evermore, and I have the keys to death and Hades."

The figure seven in the Bible is symbolic of all, complete, thus the seven lampstands are all churches, the one like a son of man was Christ, the golden girdle is symbolic of his worth, his white hair, purity; his eyes of fire, all-consuming, missing nothing; bronze feet represent strength, if they were clay it would represent a weak person; his voice like many waters, represents authority; the seven stars in his right hand represent the seven angels of the churches; the two-edged sword represents the truth, a forked tongue represents a liar; his face was like the sun in full strength, representing the light of the world.

Christ forms the foundation of the church and those who abide in Him are the building blocks, and as John said, "Do not love the world or the things in the world. If any one loves the world, love for the Father is not in him. The world passes away and the lust of it; but he who does the will of God abides forever. Who is a liar but he who denies that Jesus is the Christ, no one who denies the Son has the Father. He who confesses the Son has the father also. And this is what He promised to us, eternal life. I wrote this to you about those who would deceive you, but the anointing which you receive from Him abides in you, and you have no need that anyone should teach you (falsely) as His anointing teaches you about everything, and it is true, and is no lie, just as it has taught you, abide in Him. Little children, let us not love in word or speech, but in deed and in truth, if our hearts do not condemn us, we have confidence before God and this is His commandment that we should believe in the name of His Son Jesus Christ and love one another, just as He commanded us, and this is the testimony, that God gave us eternal life and this is in the Son, he who has the Son has life, he who has not the Son has not life."

We are confronted with the question, "To what church shall I belong, whom shall I follow?" and when we contemplate the results, the alternatives, the choice is not difficult to make. *He is the cornerstone of the church, we the building blocks, and together we shall build a holy temple unto the Lord.* Organized religioun is merely the tool through which God tries to work, until she is filled with apostasy, then she is abandoned. (Rev.) *The true church, on the other hand, includes all believers in Christ.* Many places in the New Testament speak of those who are joined to Christ, the head of the body; in other words, Christ is head of the true church. "He is also the head of the body, the church." (Colossians).

"For even as the body is one, and yet as many members, and all the members of the body, though they are many, are one body, so also is Christ. For by one Spirit we were all baptized into one body, whether Jews or Greeks, whether slaves or free, and we were all made to drink of one Spirit." (I Corinthians)

The church is comprised of those who are in Christ, and He is the cornerstone. It is not made of brick and stone and glass, that is merely the vehicle, but is made of persons who accept Christ as the Son of God and who place their trust and lives in Him, and who are set into the temple walls. To what church shall we say we belong?

VIII

Jesus Christ

One of the dilemmas that most of us face is that we feel that there is something basically wrong with us. We strive to do good at all times, but constantly backslide and yield to tempations. The ends we go to to justify what we do are almost unbelievable. Yet we know that we are constantly being defeated, and we know that this defeat can be for all eternity. This knowledge, of course, tends to cause us to develop guilt complexes, and we not only fear that we have done wrong, but that maybe we are wrong.

This knowledge causes us to come to a conviction that, no matter how hard we try, we cannot make ourselves do right. We find ourselves in a predicament, because we know that what we do depends upon ourselves, yet it is we who do wrong! This predicament can be compared to someone who has fallen into quicksand. He at once knows that he has made a wrong step and that by so doing he is now ensnared in the sand. He knows what he should have done and he knows that somehow he must get back on solid ground. But every move he makes to save himself only results in making matters worse. His very efforts cause the sand to suck him down towards destruction. Then he comes to the realization that there is absolutely nothing that he can do to save himself, and his only hope is to cry out for help, upon someone he can depend upon to pull him from the sand. And so it is with the quicksand of life. We must call out to someone upon whom we can depend to pull us out from the fatal situation that we find ourselves in. *And for the Christian, that Man is Christ.* But before we can call upon Him, we must have faith that He is what he says He is.

The Jewish people had no lack of evidence that Christ said He was the Son of God. But they rejected His testimony, even to end end. Luke wrote, "Then the whole company of them arose, and brought Him before Pilate. And they began to accuse Him saying, 'We found this man perverting our nation, and forbidding us to give tribute to Caesar, saying that He Himself is Christ the King.' And Pilate asked Him, 'Are you the King of the Jews?' and He asnwered him, 'You have said so.' And Pilate said to the chief priests and the multitudes, 'I find no crime in this man.' But they were urgent, saying, 'He stirs up the people, teaching throughout all Judea, from Galilee even to this place.' "

The Jews knew who Christ said He was, but they rejected Him. They complained that He stirred them up. To this very day He stirs us up. He disturbs us because it would be much easier if we had not heard His teachings, if He had not given us the laws of ethical and moral behavior. But He did, and it stirs us up. In trying to turn our backs on what He told us, how we ought to live, we seek justification for our acts and slip ever deeper into the quicksand.

The Jews faced Him squarely and demanded His life rather than follow His teachings. Even though they knew He was innocent, they wanted His life and demanded that He be crucified. They turned their backs upon the insistence of Pilate that Jesus was innocent, and Pilate said, "You brought me this man as one who was perverting people, and after examining Him before you, behold, I did not find this man guilty of any of your charges against Him; neither did Herod, for he sent Him back to us. Behold, nothing deserving death has been done by Him, I will therefore chastise him and release him." But they all cried out together, "Away with Him, crucify Him."

Today we often turn our backs on Him, and in our hearts crucify Him, reject Him, and, leaning upon our own selves, struggle and sink deeper into the quicksand of life.

You will recall that when the soldiers came to arrest Christ, all of the disciples forsook Him and fled. *Many of us flee before His words rather than struggle to abide by them.* But others, as did the disciples, return to Him for salvation when they realize that they cannot extricate themselves from the quicksand. They turn to Him because they recall the resurrection and remember that *the cross was not the end, but the beginning of life.* The beginning of eternity, and they call out to Him for help and are not denied.

The first and primary thing that we ought to do when we call out to Christ is to stop justifying our wrongs. We ought to stop saying that our attitudes and deeds are not as bad as what other people do, we aren't really so bad, and substitute instead a positive attitude that we could have done better and that we can do better, because when we are confronted with the cross there are no alternatives, excuses, or justifications. An innocent man was murdered on the cross, and the act cannot be justified. No evil, in the final analysis, can be justified. We may excuse it by asking, "How do we know what is good and what is evil?" when we, if we are honest with ourselves, already know. We may try to convince ourselves that we do not; but inwardly we really know. If we say that we do not know the difference then why the question? There must be doubt, and doubt cannot remain but must be resolved.

We all find ourselves floundering in the quicksand of life, and it is only when we really believe that Christ died for us that we can call upon Him to save us. Man is bound under law, and our struggles to obey the law are pitiful, for though many struggle mightily they fail through human weakness and it is for those that Christ died. We struggle to obey, but fail because we are bound under all the law, not just a part of it, and for those who fail, who struggle to keep the law, but fail, Christ died. If one struggles to obey the law and fails, if he will but accept Christ then he shall be saved. If anyone does not struggle against evil, and also rejects Christ, then he is held fully accountable under the law and must pay the resultant penalty. If we break God's laws we stand condemned under it, and if we stand upon our own convictions we are doomed to failure. All we need do is accept Christ's payment on the cross for our sins and we are set free from the law of sin and death. Paul said, "Thanks be to God through Jesus Christ our Lord. So then, I of myself serve the law of God with my mind, but with my flesh I serve the law of sin. There is therefore now no condemnation for those who are in Jesus Christ. For the law of the spirit of life in Christ Jesus has set me free from the law of sin and death."

The great thing that happened as a result of the cross, the one thing that gives us hope and changes our lives, *is not the death of Christ, but the resurrection*, proof and promise of life, not death! When Christ died, despair descended upon His followers. But when He rose from the dead, they were raised to new heights, full of new hope, and their visions did not extend only to the stars, but to the whole universe. Today, men look to conquer the stars, to go to the moon, to Mars, and beyond. They are confined in cramped vehicles, floating alone in space, faced with dangers and with a hope that they will return. But those who believe in Christ look to the whole universe; not in cramped vehicles but free; not facing dangers, but peace; not with the hope of return but with the hope of free travel throughout all of God's creation; not alone but with loved ones, and in the company of the one Man who died for us so that we might find life!

We need do more than merely believe in Christ. We must also have faith in Him, in what He said, and in the fact that if we call upon Him to pull us up on the dry land, that He will do so. Christ said, "Not everyone who says to me, 'Lord, Lord' shall enter the kingdom of heaven, but he who does the will of my Father who is in heaven." With the acceptance of Christ comes the responsibility of struggling to obey the Father, of doing good works, for good works' sake, and for no other reason. It is not easy for one to follow Christ in a simple belief in His saving grace, for He said, "Enter by the narrow gate, for the gate is wide and the way is easy that leads to destruction, and those who enter it are many. For the gate is narrow and the way is hard, that leads to life, and those who find it are few." The Christians must lead a life of living faith, not one of just mouthing off about the love of God.

Being a Christian is not easy and demands a constant struggle to maintain our beliefs in the face of all that occurs about us. Sometimes the struggles seem almost unbearable. We cannot suffer the loss of loved ones, we cannot watch struggling humanity and not suffer a little ourselves. Evil seems to be at every hand. Temptation is everywhere and we grow weary. Then we remember the words of Christ, "Come to me, all who labor and are heavy laden, and I will give you rest. Take my yoke upon you and learn from Me; for I am gentle and lowly in heart, and you will find rest for your souls. For my yoke is easy, and my burden is light."

Sometimes we are a little too hard on ourselves. We worry about the little white lies we tell, about the little fibs. We wonder if we have too much, and if we give enough to charity. We stew a lot about little things, about the past; we fret about the future, and we are not sure of salvation because we constantly breach the laws of God, sometimes inadvertently, sometimes on purpose. But we err when we think we ought to be perfect. We are extolled only to be "acceptable in the eyes of God." We condemn ourselves too quickly, and too severely. The evil ones are men like those in the Mafia, gamblers, dope peddlers, murderers, those who live at night, in darkened places, who prowl our alleys and streets, bent upon murder and robbery, those who plot wars, and who do all manner of evil. Evil men with evil hearts! These are the ones who stand under condemnation. Responsible citizens who strive diligently to do good, but sometimes fail, who commit errors in judgment, who lack wisdom to solve evils, and who yield to human frailties and weaknesses, need not be as hard on themselves as some people are. *We are not perfect; if we were, we would not need Christ.* God knows this and, being a God of love, He does not always condemn us for what we condemn ourselves for. Too much self-condemnation is not a healthy thing. We need first ask, what was our intent? Did we mean to hurt someone? Could we help ourselves at the time? Did we with malice aforethought contrive to violate any of the Ten Commandments, or did it just happen through, perhaps, thoughtlessness or carelessness? If you are looking for perfection, you will surely fail, but if you look for forgiveness, you will surely succeed.

Those who accept the death of Christ as payment for our sins experience a change in their lives. They become different people. Paul taught, "Therefore, since we are justified by faith we have peace with God through our Lord Jesus Christ. Through HIm we have obtained access to this grace in which we stand, and we rejoice in our hope of sharing the glory of God. More than that, we rejoice in our sufferings, knowing that suffering produces endurance, and endurance produces character, and character produces hope, and hope does not disappoint us, because God's love has been poured into our hearts through the Holy Spirit which has been given to us. While we were yet helpless, at the right time Christ died for the ungodly."

When we face the cross we are faced with a decision that places us squarely before God, *and we must make a choice*; to accept the payment His Son made, or to reject it. This, in turn, forces us to decide what our lives will be like, our destiny, both in an absolute sense. We can choose the world or take the new life that is offered us through Christ. We are called to do more than just "be good"; we are called upon to be followers of Christ, and to strive to live by His teachings. It is easy to assume that if we do wrong, then to save ourselves all we need to do is to be better. But it is not enough. We must strive to live as did Christ, in relation to one's fellow man.

The choice we make is to resist sin and death and take life. *It is a life and death decision!* If you think upon it for a moment, you will see that it is the most important decision that you will ever make. We think that the decision to marry is a difficult one. The decision to change jobs. The decision to permit the surgeon to operate upon ourselves or our loved ones. These are hard decisions to make, but they deal in matters temporary. In the decision to accept the death of Christ as being for us, and then to live in accordance with that decision is most difficult. Many of us think that we have already made a decision, but take a look at it; would we take a firm position and state, "I make the decision to follow Christ and from this day forward I shall not yield to any temptation that comes my way, upon pain of death!" Or, should we say, "I shall make the decision to follow Christ, and *with His help* I shall from this day forward resist evil, to the best of my abilities, with the fervent prayer that when I slip, and I know I shall, that he will forgive me for my sins?" Here we make the decision honestly, because we all know that we are not perfect, we are not strong enough to resist all evils that come our way, but with the help of Christ there is hope, because it was for us, the sinners, that Christ died.

Thus the decision is difficult, for each must choose for or against God's saving grace enacted upon the cross. To procrastinate, and refuse or postpone the decision, is of itself a choice of destiny. By our choice we decree beforehand our own fate! Not just for a short time, it is not a now-or-never decision, *but a now-and-forever decision*! What an awesome responsibility!

So we find mankind struggling to resist evil, to obey the law, and in his weakness failing; then we see God, in his mercy, providing another way for us. If we struggle and fail but accept Christ's payment upon the cross as genuine, we shall nevertheless be saved. And having accepted this we must strive to live lives patterned after Him. The reward is everlasting life, basking in the love of God, free at last from the laws of sin and death and, as stated in Revelation, "Behold, the dwelling place of God is with men. He will dwell with them, and they shall be His people, and God Himself will be with them, He will wipe away every tear from their eyes, and death shall be no more, neither shall there be mourning nor crying or pain any more for the former things have passed away."

The only description which exists as to what Christ looked like is contained in the Apocrypha which is a compilation of fourteen books which were omitted from the King James Version of the Bible. These Books were formerly included in the Authorized Version and were written at about the same time as were the other Scriptures, but they are now generally omitted. They were printed for decades between the Old Testament and the New. At one time the Church of England prohibited their omission from any edition of the Bible. In 1827 they were excluded from all printed Bibles, although they are still printed in the Vulgate Bible used by the Roman Catholic Church. Nevertheless, the description is so vivid and descriptive of the paintings and sculptures which adorn our Churches that it is worhy of presenting here:

"There hath appeared in these times, and still is, a man of great power named Jesus Christ, who is called by the Gentiles the prophet of truth, whom his disciples call the Son of God: raising the dead and healing diseases, a man in stature middling tall, and comely, having a revered countenance, which they that look upon may love and fear; having hair of the hue of an unripe hazelnut and smooth down to his ears, but from the ears in curling locks somewhat darker and more shining, waving over his shoulders; having a parting at the middle of the head according to the fashion of the Nazareans; a brow smooth and very calm, with a face without wrinkle or any blemish, which a moderate color makes beautiful; with a nose and mouth no fault at all can be found; having a full beard of the color of his hair, not long, but a little forked at the chin; having an expression simple and mature, the eyes grey, glancing, and clear; in rebuke terrible, in admonition kind and lovable, cheerful yet keeping gravity; sometimes he has wept, but never laughed; in stature of body tall and straight, with hands and arms fair to look upon; in talk grave, reserved and modest, so that he was rightly called by the prophet fairer than the children of men."

IX

The Living Christ

One of the most difficult things for many is the acceptance, in a literal sense, that Christ actually rose from the dead and ascended into heaven. There are those who take the view that the resurrection was spiritual, that is, that His memory and influence continued with His disciples. In carrying on His work, they continued His "life," or "spirit," on the earth. *We should reject this view because it is contrary to Scripture*; it is merely a way of trying to explain that which is difficult to believe. It is rationalizing one's thoughts, or, in fact, apoligizing for one's beliefs. We should not apologize to any man!

There is a basic difference between our cross and the cross presented by the Catholic Church. Their cross always depicts Christ hanging on the cross. Our cross is empty. The empty cross depicts the fact that He is not there! He has risen, He does not hang on the cross! We do not look upon a cross showing Jesus hanging on it, but to the empty cross and to the empty tomb, for He has risen, He lives! He is not there!

Let us take a look at the Scriptures, and here again we must take the position that if one takes any part of the Scriptures and throws them out, they might just as well throw away the rest; for to discredit one part discredits the credibility of it all!

The account of the resurrection according to Matthew: "Now after the Sabbath, towards the dawn of the first day of the week, Mary Magdalene and the other Mary went to see the sepulcher. And behold, there was a great earthquake, for an angel of the Lord descended from heaven and came and rolled back the stone, and sat upon it. His appearance was like lightning, and his raiment white as snow. And for fear of him the guards trembled and became like dead men, but the angel of the Lord said to the women, 'Do not be afraid for I know that you seek Jesus who was crucified. He is not there; for He has risen, as He said. Come, see the place where He lay. Then go quickly and tell His disciples that He has risen from the dead, and behold, He is going before you to Galilee; there you will see Him. Lo, I have told you. So they departed quickly from the tomb with fear and great joy, and ran to tell his disciples. And behold, Jesus met them and said, 'Hail.' And they came up and took hold of His feet and worshipped him. Then Jesus said to them, 'Do not be afraid; go tell my breathren to go to Galilee, and there they will see me.'

When the two Marys peered into the tomb, Christ was not there, because He had risen. They were the first to see Him, to speak to Him, and to touch Him, when they worshipped at His feet. This story has been told too often, believed by too many people, *to have just been concocted from someone's imagination!*

Then Matthew continued, "Now the eleven disciples went to Galilee, to the mountain to which Jesus had directed them. And when they saw him they worshipped Him; but some doubted. And Jesus said to them, 'All authority in heaven and on earth has been given to me. Go therefore and make disciples to all nations, baptizing them in the name of the Father, and of the Son, and of the Holy Spirit, teaching them to observe all that I have commanded you; and lo, I am with you always, to the close of the age.' "

So the two Marys saw Him, and the twelve disciples, yet some doubted. To this very day some still doubt. Some will always doubt, simply because they cannot grasp the wonder of it. It is beyond their comprehension. To quote Shakespeare, "Ah, what fools these mortals be."

Matthew, Mark, Luke, and John all record the resurrection. Their versions differ, and the words spoken differ, but the message is the same: "He is not here, He has risen." It is doubtful if any four men could have recorded these events in exactly the same way, anymore than we would expect four people to witness the second coming of Christ and tell the story in the same way. *The indisputable fact is that all testified that He had risen*, that He was seen with Mary, that He talked to the disciples, that he talked to the men on the road, that He taught the multitudes. Are we as bad as Thomas? Must we place our hand in the wound of His side, our fingers in His pierced hands? And if we did, would we still believe? Might we not say that surely I must be losing my mind; I dreamed that I touched the wound in Jesus' side and felt the nail holes in His hands! *How long do you think it would take for you to discount it all as an illusion?* How many of your friends would believe you? If you insisted upon such a position, they would have the men in the little white coats looking for you. What then? Faith!

But faith alone is not enough. We must strive to follow in His footsteps. *How easy it is to settle for a memory.* We give honor to a Jesus who lived long ago and far away. But if we settle for just His memory, if we merely believe in His reality and tell no man, nor do any good works, then He just might as well have remained in the tomb!

The event of the resurrection has been the center of debates and endless questions through the centuries. It is easy for us to accept the fact that He was crucified. This gives us no problem. Yet this event is likewise recorded in the Bible, by the same writers who wrote about the resurrection. Why is it so easy to believe what we read about His death? Perhaps that, too, was a figment of someone's imagination. Why is this any more credible than the resurrection? *Both events are written in the same book by the same writers.* Did they tell the truth about His death? A lie about His resurrection?

It doesn't make sense. It would have been much simpler to just have recorded His crucificion and then closed the account with the words, "And then it is supposed that He went unto the Father," but they did not! They recorded the events. Who saw Him, what He said, and all the rest. But some say, "Let's take our pens and strike all of that out; the rest is true, but this is false!" Many take the position, "Let's strike it all out and go our merry way. If we strike out the resurrection, then the rest is not valid either, so let's just forget it all." But we should say, *"Strike not a single word!"*

We do not worship a dead God, but a living Christ, and as such become a part of His glory. When we do then as written in 2 Ephesians, "So then you are no longer strangers and sojourners, but you are fellow citizens with the Saints and members of the household of God, built upon the foundation of the Apostles and prophets, Christ Jesus, Himself being the chief cornerstone, in whom the whole structure is joined together and grows into a holy temple in the Lord, in whom you also are built into it, for a dwelling place of God in the Spirit." What this is saying is that we are a part of the temple of God, and a member of His household. Can one dream dreams greater than this? No, we cannot look back to the empty tomb; we must share now the "newness of life, through the risen Christ."

If we truly believe in the risen Christ, then we can tolerate all the hurts that life can give us; we can withstand the onslaughts of evil; we can lose loved ones without questioning why; because we have the utmost faith in the living God. That He has risen, and if this is true, then His promises are true, and we, too, shall one day rise to be rejoined by those who have died before us, and we shall ask no more the question . . . why? We should not be ashamed to say, "I do not know why, I do not understand it. But then, neither do I understand why they crucified Christ. So I leave those answers to the living God until another day. Then I will know, but in the interim I shall not while away the years in grief at the loss of a loved one, but in joy at the knowledge that these things of the earth are of a temporary nature."

We cling to the song we sing so often, "I'm standing on the promises of God!" Do you know anything better upon which to stand?

There is a passage in Ephesians which gives us counsel that we not blame God, that we not blame life, that we do not blame others, and it reads: "Let all bitterness and wrath and anger and clamor and slander be put away from you, with all malice, and be kind to one another, tender-hearted, forgiving one another, as God in Christ forgave you. Therefore be imitators of God, as beloved children, and walk in love, as Christ loved us and gave Himself up for us."

The biblical account of the resurrection is most difficult, and one of the reasons is that until one becomes clearly aware of the living god, until they sense His presence, *their intellects are behind their emotions.* We may have emotional feelings, but can we intellectually accept what we feel? How long does it take to learn something of great significance? A lifetime? All through His ministry, according to Luke, Jesus had made references to Old Testament prophecies, indicating that they were being fulfilled in the sight and hearing of the apostles. Yet the truth failed to sink into their consciousness. It was only after His death and resurrection that they finally saw the truth of what He was telling them. Many times in our lives, something happens that jolts us and our minds are opened. It is then that we come to a real understanding of what happened upon the cross, and afterwards. Sometimes we become so involved in our grief that the message does not come through, but when it does, then there is, as the apostles often said, "great joy and blessings for God." No matter the cause of our former grief!

But don't feel bad if you have difficulty with the resurrection, because the disciples did also. They knew that dead men did not walk again, they were intelligent men aware of the laws of nature. They were utterly unable to cope with the facts when Jesus appeared before them. It was only after talking with HIm, touching Him, and listening to Him that they were able to put together the pieces and believe. When they believed, then the Holy Spirit entered into them and they dedicated the rest of their lives to Him.

Fact and Fiction are not the same, they are diametrically opposed. *Fiction dies, but fact cannot die.* A fact is a fact and saying otherwise does not make it otherwise. It cannot be stamped out nor pushed into the background to be buried for all time. Many have tried to stamp out the story of the resurrection. To bury it. To have men forget it. To accept it as false. But the fact of His recurrection has withstood all onslaughts. This, in and of itself, apart from the resurrection, is a miracle. No story in history has had such massive attempts made to stamp it out. To discredit. To belie, as has the story of Jesus, His life, His death, and His resurrection. All were doomed to failure and each attempt served only to strengthen the facts. Kings tried to stamp it out. Great rulers' armies were raised against it. Believers were tortured and killed, but when the dust settles, each time one man survives and His name is Jesus Christ. We could probably name on our hands the number of rulers that we can remember, most of them in the twentieth century. Many have risen, called themselves gods, thought themselves above mere humanity, but all have slipped into oblivion in the memory of man. *Not so with the living Christ, because He is not dead, He lives in the twentieth century, so is not forgotten and His name is in the hearts and on the tongues of millions, and they speak of a living Christ!* There has been none like Him, nor shall there ever be, and this fact alone is enough to increase my belief in Him and in the resurrection.

When anyone finds Christ, do not be amazed, either for him or for yourselves, for as Mark recorded, the angel at the tomb said, "Do not be amazed, you seek Jesus of Nazareth, who was crucified. He has risen, He is not here; see the places where they laid Him. But go, tell His disciples and Peter that He is going before you to Galilee; there you will see Him, as He told you."

Christ long ago left Galilee, and has gone unto all the world, and you might meet Him any day, at any time, or maybe you already have. And if you have, you are among the greatest of the great because you walk with the living God.

X

The Resurrection

We are all familiar with the death and resurrection of Christ. No story in history has ever been told so often, nor heard by so many people. Once each year the church focuses upon it, and one day each year we gather together as on no other day. That day is, of course, Easter Sunday. The dictionary defines Easter as "an annual Christian festival in commemoration of the resurrection of Jesus Christ, observed on the first Sunday after the full moon that occurs on or next after March 21." *That may well be the technical definition of Easter, but to the Christian it means much more.* The resurrection of Christ contains the promise of eternal life, and also assures us of the continuing presence of the living Lord in our midst. It is these two beliefs that Give Easter its great significance to us. Eternal life and the knowledge that He lives! The belief that He lives gives us the assurance that if He lives, then we, too, shall live.

Paul wrote in 1 Corinthians: "For I delivered to you as of first importance what I also received, that Christ died for our sins in accordance with the Scriptures, that He was buried, that He was raised on the third day in accordance with the Scriptures, and that He appeared to Cephas, then to the twelve. Then He appeared to more than 500 brethren at one time, most of whom are still alive, although some have fallen asleep. Then He appeared to James, then to all the apostles. Last of all, as to one untimely born, He appeared also to me. For I am the least of the apostles, unfit to be called an apostle, because I persecuted the church of God. But by the grace of God I am what I am, and His grace towards me was not in vain. On the contrary, I worked harder than any of them, though it was not I, but the grace of God which is with me. Whether then it was I or they, so we preach and so you believed.

"Now if Christ is preached as raised from the dead, how can some of you say that there is no resurrection of the dead? But if there is no resurrection of the dead, then Christ has not been raised; if Christ has not been raised, then our preaching is in vain and your faith is in vain. We are even found to be misrepresenting God, because we testified of God that he raised

Christ, whom He did not raise if it is true that the dead are not raised. For if the dead are not raised, then Christ has not been raised. If Christ has not been raised, your faith is futile and you are still in your sins. Then those also who have fallen asleep in Christ have perished. If for this life only we have hoped in Christ, we are of all men most to be pitied.''

Indeed, we are to be pitied, if the resurrection is a myth and the accounts of it fradulent. But we, through the grace of God, know that it is no myth, and we know that the account is true. It is those who do not believe who are to be pitied, because they never had the supreme revelation of the resurrection of Christ, nor do they sense His living presence in the world. How lonely they must be, standing alone in the universe, without hope, without love and without peace. To them Easter is just another Sunday, another day of living and nothing more, but to us when the sun rises and the dawn of another Easter is here, we feel His presence and we know that He is our Lord and that He is Lord of the universe. We do not think only of the words of John, ''Repent and be baptized,'' But we revel in the fact that salvation has been won through the death, burial, and resurrection of Jesus, the Son of God. Then we repent of our own accord and not as the result of prodding, and we are freely baptized in the power of the Holy Spirit!

The power of the resurrection continues to live in generation after generation of Christians, for they feel the compelling presence of the living God. As world travel becomes easier and faster, it is simpler to spread the word of God to the ends of the world. Paul spoke of the ''Christ who lives in me.'' When the Christian travels, those who come into contact with him are aware that something is different about them. When Christ lives in a person His presence radiates from that person and all who come into contact with him are aware of that radiance. *This does not apply to the professing Christians or to a denominational church member, but to those in whom Christ dwells, to those whom the Holy Spirit has descended, and who, without reservation, has accepted Christ as Saviour.*

A person who believes that a resurrection is an impossibility cannot accept the truth of the resurrection. One must first believe that God has the power to raise persons from the dead before he can believe in either the resurrected Lord or in any possibility that they, too, can be raised from the dead by that same power. They have little difficulty in believing that He has the power to take two small cells and raise a life from out of the dust, but they cannot believe that when those same cells return to the dust that the life which came into being with it can survive without the dust. Yet the dust is nothing; the person who dwells within is real, it is the spirit that dwells in the dust that does not return to dust, for it came not from the dust but from God and to God it will return, if it is worthy of His acceptance and love.

Christ Himself rose up from the dust into life and He, too, returned to the dust, but His spirit was worthy and was loved and He was resurrected to reunite with the God who sent it into the world. If this be true then we, too, if we are worthy, will return unto the Father when our flesh has been returned to dust. Believe this and the joys of heaven will abound in you forever.

The resurrection of Jesus continues to be the most important single event in the history of mankind for the following reasons: first, the resurrection confirms the significance of the life of Jesus. Without it His life would never have been understood as the actual presence of God in the world (the incarnation). Since belief in the incarnation is basic to Christian theology, the resurrection becomes the central fact of Christian belief. *When belief in the resurrection begins to wither, faith begins to decline.* Only as long as one believes that Christ has risen is he able to maintain his faith and works. As Paul said, "Your faith is futile, and you are still in your sins," without the belief in the resurrection.

Second, the resurrection is the source of Christian strength. In a world of violence, injustice, intemperance and inhumanity, despair is easy and the maintenance of hope difficult. But the belief in the final triumph of good over evil, of life over death, is man's greatest hope. The resurrection of Christ proves that our hopes are not vain, but are fulfilled.

Finally, the resurrection gives assurance in times of death and personal insecurity about life and death, per se. Christ said through John, "Because I live, you will live also." This assurance *enables the Christian* to feel secure in an insecure world, and he develops a conviction of the ultimate victory of life over death, good over evil, and hate melts away; love prevails. We believe the truth of what Christ said, "Because I live, you will live also." It is an impertinence to believe otherwise.

Let us see if we can capsulize the meaning of the resurrection: We are born under the law of sin and death, bound under the whole law. As human-beings we have not the strength to abide by the law, the flesh is weak. We are prisoners of Satan under the power of evil. Christ comes into the world and sets us free from the law of sin and death, and redeems us from the power of Satan and sets us free. Under law we were condemned to death for we breached the law; under Christ we are set free from the law of sin and death and come under life. *Christ gave His life so that we might live,* and all that is required of us is that we accept His payment and believe in Him. The crucifixion was His payment, life for death, so that all might have life. It was an act of love, for God so loved the world that He gave His only begotten Son that we might have life. When we accept Christ we have life and, having accepted, can do only good works because we cannot do otherwise. If Christ dwells within us and we in Him, good works will surely follow. Good works do not precede salvation, they follow it. Good works demand pay; love does not demand anything but love. Good works done out of love expects nothing in return. Righteousness is a gift of God out of love in return for love; it is no reward, it is a free gift. Christ freely gave His life upon the cross so that we might have life. Greater love has no man than this. The resurrection was the victory of Christ over death and He offers to us an opportunity to share that victory upon the mere belief in one thing: "Whosoever liveth and believeth in me, though he be dead, yet shall he live."

We hear more and more about the doctrine of reincarnation and more and more books are being written on the subject. It is difficult to believe that the doctrine of reincarnation is within the meaning of everlasting life, because when we speak of living with Christ, that is exactly what we mean. *To be born in pain, to dread to die, over and over again, cannot be fair nor just.* We have been born, and if the purpose of the reincarnation is to purify the spirit, *then let us purify ours in this one life.* If they are wrong and we are right, there will be no second chance for me or for you; let us not gamble with our souls. If time is required to purify the soul, *then extend our one life,* but do not let us cause the pain of motherhood to occur over and over, and perhaps now and then cause a woman's death while trying to give us another chance to purify a life which we cannot even remember with the conscious mind. To be born a worm, then a mouse, then a dog, then a cow and finally a human, to be born over and over is such a waste of effort. *Consider how many have traveled that imaginary route to wind up miserable, stupid human beings, instead of something noble.*

Christ said that He goes unto the Father and that He goes to prepare a place for us and that He will come again and gather us into His household. This we believe, and it is this upon which we will commit our life, our trust, and our faith—not upon the rantings of distorted minds who produce not a single shred of evidence upon which to base their theories except visions and hallucinations. *We have the evidence.* Christ was seen in life, He was seen in death, He was seen after death. These are not daydreams of those who dream up doctrines, when they already have fulfillment of the greatest dream that dreamers could ever possibly imagine. Why do men seek better ways, when the way to eternal life has already been shown? Why do they conjure up new theories when they already have fact and truth? When Christ said, "I am the way, the truth, and the light," why do men imagine other ways, and having done so, seek to lead other men down their false paths which they seek to widen? The way is narrow when one goes down the true path of salvation.

Peter speaks of these people who put forward such doctrines when he wrote:

But like irrational animals, creatures of instinct, born to be caught and killed, reveling in matters of which they are ignorant, they count it a pleasure to revel in their dissipation, carousing with you. They have eyes full of adultery, insatiable for sin. They intice unsteady souls. They have hearts trained in greed. Accursed children! Forsaking the right way, they have gone astray, they have followed the way of Balaam, who loved gain from wrongdoing. These are waterless springs and mists driven by the storm, uttering folly, they entice with passion the flesh of men who have barely

escaped from those who live in error. They promise freedom, but they themselves
are slaves to corruption, for whatever overcomes a man, by that they are enslaved.
The dog turns back to its own vomit, and the sow is washed only to wallow in the
mire.''

What an indictment!

We should not stand upon the teachings of men, nor should we attend
their doctrines, because God's word spoken through Christ is enough. There
is no greater authority, nor is there any living person or any dead man whose
lips have long been stopped with dust, upon whom we can place our trust,
our lives, and our souls, but we rely upon the risen Lord and in Him, and
by Him alone will we stand steadfast. He died for us and we shall try to
live for Him. What modern man believes his own rubbish so strongly that
he would lay down his life in belief of it, or so that we might believe in
his doctrine? Yet, our Lord did. He laid down His life for us. He came into
the world, He taught us, He died for us, and then returned unto the Father
with a promise that He would come again for us. What more can the heart
desire? There is an anguish in our hearts when we hear men try to circum-
vent, to alter, to downgrade and to modify the greatest truth that has ever
been revealed to the hearts of men.

What did Jesus say? "I am the way . . . " No other way for the Christian, one way, no maybes, no qualification, but a simple statement of fact.
Then He said, "and the truth . . . " He is the truth, no other teaching,
but He alone stands as the truth. Once more a simple statement of fact.
Then He continues, "and the light." He is the light, we are enlightened
through Him, not through silly doctrines, false teachings, dreams and
hallucinations. Men see the light when they know Christ. Another simple
statement. So let's put it all back together—"I am the way, and the truth,
and the light." How very simple, how very uncomplicated. *Its simplicity
testifies of itself and the truth of it.* When Mary left the empty tomb she
was crying, "They have taken away my Lord, and I know not where to find
Him." The modern writers are doing the same, they are trying to take away
our Lord so that we will not know where to find Him. But Mary found
Him, and so shall we. Christ was speaking to His followers, to those who
are now known as Christians. *God has spoken to other men, in other ages,
in other lands*, so that they, too, might have His love, *but Christ was speaking to us when He said, "I am the way."*

The greatest words that can ever be understood are the words contained
in the Holy Scriptures and the words spoken by Jesus himself if it be one's
desire to present himself as worthy before God. We have found no fault
with Scripture and, when it comes to a matter of religion, one needs look
no further for wisdom. To do otherwise is foolishness. One great fact stands
out above all other teachings: "Christ was crucified, dead and buried, on
the third day He arose from the dead and ascended into heaven." Christ

said he would return and come for us. We believe Him. We are convinced that He will come for us, to the last lost sheep, and gather us unto His own. If this is not so ,then we are to be pitied most, above all other men.

We should each vow that no man shall ever hear our anguished cry, "They have taken away our Lord, and we know not where to find Him," for we have found Him.

XI

Eternal Life

The attainment of eternal life is the hope of most of the religions of the world and for the Christian, it is the pinnacle of his religion. Religion has as its ultimate end the destruction of the world, as we now know it, and the creation of a new world. We believe that there will be an end to life as we now know it, and that there will be a new life, and that all things will pass away into a new state of being.

John, in the Book of Revelations, wrote: "Then I saw a new heaven and a new earth; for the first heaven and the first earth has passed away, and the sea was no more. And I saw the holy city, new Jerusalem, coming down out of heaven from God, prepared as a bride adorned for her husband; and I heard a great voice from the throne saying, 'Behold . . . he will wipe away every tear from their eyes, and death shall be no more, neither shall there be mourning nor crying nor pain any more, for the former things have passed away.' "

We are the sole possessors of the beliefs to which we hold, and to the opinions that we hold true. These opinions are arrived at independently, and are often formed only by arriving at them through intellectual conclusions, and not based upon fact nor proof. We cannot always explain why or how we come to a certain belief, but we are aware that through reading, group discussions, experience, tradition and biblical studies, we do arrive at a conviction, even though we have never observed the very thing that we believe in. *It is also impossible for the human mind to conceive a state of not being.* We are, and we cannot conceive that we might some day not be. It is the nature of all living things to desire to always be. We do exist, and to suppose that one day we will not exist is to suppose something that is self-contradictory. All that has been said about heaven, though it cannot be investigated by reason, nor proven by fact, must not forthwith be rejected as false, for although no man can come forth with proof of heaven, no man can come forward with disproof of its reality.

The existence of heaven is one of the few things that one can come to a belief in, even though he has little understanding of its essence. Human intellect is incapable of being able to comprehend just what heaven will really be like.

The choice of a belief in a heaven is really quite simple—*one either believes that there is a heavn or that there is not a heaven. There are no other possibilities*. If there is no heaven then no harm can come to those who hold to either belief, for neither will ever be aware of the truth or falseness of it. On the other hand, if there is a heaven, then one will find his fondest dreams fulfilled, while the other will rue the day he rejected it. It's a little bit like playing Russian Roulette—the loser loses all.

The belief in reincarnation and in transmigration is not a denial of eternal life, for the ultimate end, after many lives, the soul is supposed to reach a state of perfection and then enters into a oneness with God, or is absorbed into the oneness of God and becomes a part of it. Thus it is immortal, although it loses its identity. Exactly what is accomplished by this? If indeed it is accomplished, it is difficult to grasp, *for it appears to be without ultimate purpose*. We believe that we retain our identify and our own individuality after death and that, based upon the kinds of lives we live, we will be received into heaven or into hell, there to dwell for all eternity.

Most persons have no conscious desire to die. In their minds they are willing to continue as they are and to improve their lot here on earth. Yet each person knows that he was born to die, and many, if not most (out of sheer boredom), might eventually wish to die, regardless of the consequences, even if he could live forever. Most people picture a heaven for themselves, one that will be free of the trials and tribulations of this earth, and that they will be able to pursue that which gives them joy on this earth. Every man forms a mental picture of heaven. There are probably as many concepts of heaven as there are minds.

Obviously, since it is impossible to reason on a subject that is unknown, the acceptance of heaven must be taken mostly on hope, on faith, and on desire. All religions have offered a promise of eternal life of some kind or another, and in most cases, a hell of some kind or another, but most have not offered an adequate description of what they are really like. The kind of heaven is left to each imagination, and it has been the case from the beginning of time.

Christ described the attainment of heaven in these ways:

"The kingdom of heaven is like a grain of mustard seed, which a man took and sowed into his field; it is the smallest of all seeds, but when it has grown it is the greatest of all shrubs and becomes a tree, so that the birds of the air come and make nests in its branches."

We do sometimes feel that we are the most insignificant of all creation, yet when we grow in God, we become aware of a greatness that dwells within us, and our souls, like the birds, seek to fly off into heaven.

"The kingdom of heaven is like leaven which a woman took and hid in three measures of a meal, till it was all leavened.

The kingdom of heaven is like treasure hidden in a field, which a man found and covered up, then in his joy he goes and sells all that he has and buys that field.

Again, the kingdom of heaven is like a merchant in search of fine pearls, who, on finding one pearl of great value, went and sold all that he had and bought it.

Again, the kingdom of heaven is like a net which was thrown into the sea and gathered fish of every kind, when it was full, men drew it ashore and sat down and sorted the good into vessels but threw away the bad. So it will be at the close of the age. The angels will come out and separate the evil from the righteous, and throw them into the furnace of fire, there men will weep and gnash their teeth.''

All of these parables deal with man living in the depths of life, in overcoming evil, and then rising above life's torments, with a hope of heaven and a dream of life, and not of death. The bread was buried under the flour until ready; the man who hid the treasure in the field gave up all so that he might possess it; the man who found the pearl gave all his wealth for it; and the fisherman took the good fish and kept them, but the bad ones they threw away. We are of the world, we are buried in life's problems, but if we overcome we must pay the price; what we buy is eternal life and a place in heaven. We are called upon over and over to rise up, to come out of the world into God's love. Christ lamented, "Oh, Jerusalem, Jerusalem, killing the prophets and stoning those who are sent to you! How often would I have gathered your children together as a hen gathers her brood under her wings, and you would not!''

Christ promises heaven when He says that the Son of Man will place the sheep on His right hand and the goats on the left hand, and will say to those on His right hand, "Come, oh blessed of my father, inherit the kingdom prepared for you from the foundation of the world, for I was hungry and you gave me food, I was thirsty and you gave me water, I was a stranger and you welcomed me, I was naked and you clothed me, I was sick and you visited me, I was in prison and you came to me." And when they said they could not remember doing these things, Christ said, "Truly I say to you, as you did it to one of the least of these, my brethren, you did it to me." Then he continues by condemning the evil ones, and closes with these words: "And they will go away into eternal punishment, but the righteous into eternal life."

In Romans, Paul does not try to deny the existence of evil, pain, and suffering, but makes the point that we, as Christians, can endure them because they are of no import when compared to the glory that is to come. Paul is sure that God will fulfill his promises and that it will involve all of creation. He never minimizes the fact that we all will suffer, but he insists that we must find the strength to endure, not in stoic resignation to our fate, to the inevitable, but in the assurance of the ultimate victory of God.

Paul is aware of the apparent futility of nature, which, like a great wheel, turns and returns always to the place from which it started. He speaks of the suffering of animals, of natural calamities and of disasters. But Paul says that although we are all involved in these things, we must sustain our hope of a good life in the future. We must hope for something better than that which we now possess.

Paul writes of the suffering in the world and of man and of the hope of the world, as follows:

"I consider that the sufferings of this present time are not worth comparing with the glory that is to be revealed to us. For the creation waits with eager longing for the revealing of the sons of God; for the creation was subjected to futility, not of its own will but by the will of Him who subjected it in hope; because the creation itself will be set free from its bondage to decay, and obtain the glorious liberty of the children of God. We know that the whole creation has been groaning in travail together until now; and not only the creation, but we ourselves, who have the first fruits of the Spirit, groan inwardly as we wait for adoption as sons, the redemption of our bodies. For in hope we are saved."

Revelation states, "Then the seventh angel blew his trumpet, and there were loud voices in heaven saying, 'The kingdom of the world has become the kingdom of our Lord and of His Christ, and He shall reign forever and ever.' " What this verse is saying is that the Sovereign God will, in his own time, demonstrate His sovereignty by destroying everything evil and reigning supreme in love and righteousness over all creation.

We live in perilous times and are constantly confronted by disease and death, by threats of atomic war, by increases in violent crime, dope addiction, and on and on. We sometimes feel that we are caught up in forces over which we have no control and a sense of helplessnes overwhelms us, yet when one has faith in God and believes that God is what He is, that He does what He does, and that He permits whatever happens, with the ultimate end being for the salvation of men, and believes that no matter how deficient is our understanding that all that happens comes from a good and righteous Lord, then we lose our feelings of insecurity and fear and obtain a feeling of strength and fearlessness, for if God is with us, who can be against us?

There is a story about a ship crossing the ocean in a terrible storm. For days the wind blew and the ship wallowed and tossed while the passengers cowered in fear below decks. At last they decided that one of their members should venture out and inquire of the captain whether there was any possibility of living through the storm. The man selected made his way to the captain's bridge. There he saw the captain holding to the wheel and giving orders to his crew in a firm voice. The man returned to the passengers and assured them, "I have seen the Captains face and all is well."

It is this kind of faith that can carry us through the times of death and the times in which we live, for we know that there is One who stands at the helm and guides the ship of fate, and we know that all is well.

The end of the world as we now know it, and everlasting life, together with a conviction of heaven, is prophesied throughout the Bible. Can we believe in biblical prophecies? Well, let's look at some. Prophecy is a declaration of something to come, a prediction. Let's look at some prophecies relating to Christ and to His ministry. There are many, many more that have come to pass, but time will not permit naming them all, so we shall look only at some of the prophecies relating to Christ.

Micah predicted the birthplace of Christ *700 years before his birth*: "But thou, Bethlehem, though thou be little among the thousands of Judah, yet out of thee shall He come forth . . . ''

Isaiah, *720 years before Christ was born*, predicted: "Behold, a virgin shall conceive, and bear a son, and shall call his name Immanual.''

Isaiah predicted the place of His ministry.

Isaiah predicted His power coming from God.

Isaiah predicted His saving character.

Isaiah predicted His healing character.

Isaiah predicted His use of miracles.

Isaiah predicted the inclusion of the Gentiles.

The book of Psalms predicted the zeal by which He would teach.

The giving of His word to the Jew and to the Gentile is predicted in Isaiah.

His humility is predicted in Zechariah.

His rejection is predicted in Isaiah.

Zechariah predicted that He would be deserted.

Isaiah predicted that He would be scourged and spat upon.

Psalms predicted that He would be given vinegar to drink.

Psalms predicted that His palms would be pierced by nails.

Psalms predicted that He would be forsaken by God.

Isaiah predicted that He would die surrounded by enemies.

Psalms predicted that He would agonize of thirst.

Psalms predicted that He would commend His spirit to God.

Psalms prediced that His garments would be distributed.

Psalms predicted that none of His bones would be broken.

Psalms predicted that He would rise from the dead.

Psalms predicted that He would ascend into glory.

The predictions were from 400 to 1,600 years before His birth! Christ predicted his own betrayal and said at the Last supper, "One of you will betray me." He also predicted the place, means, manner, and duration of His death before being resurrected.

There are so many prophecies in the Bible that have been fulfilled that it would take reams to describe them all. So many have come to pass that it is almost unbelievable. They have come to pass with amazing accuracy! What makes anyone think that the prophecies relating to a new world, to eternal life and to the existence of heaven, will not also come to pass? We believe that the Bible contains God's divine word; if one believes that, then he must also believe in the truth of its prophecies.

The very first prediction of the coming of Christ is in the book of Genesis where, after Adam and Eve had sinned and were driven from the Garden, God said: "And the seed of woman shall bruise the serpent's head." Well, the truth of Christ has bruised the serpent's head ever since his ministry.

When the angels cried, "Peace on earth, good will towards men" upon the birth of Christ, many thought that this prediction meant that it was to be an immediate peace. But they failed to understand that this promise did not pertain to life at or during the first coming of Christ, *but that it would come upon the second coming of Christ*. Individual peace is possible now, through faith in Christ, as a result of his first coming, but universal peace will come to the world only upon his second coming when he will rule the world. Total peace will come to man upon his own second birth, when he enters into eterntiy and brotherhood with God.

When one comes to the realization that he and all that he possesses is dependent upon God, that he is the product of the Creator, and that what is, is, and that what is to come, will come, then the debates cease and the restless heart is quiet. This does not mean dependency in the sense that one is subject to the whims of some deity, but in the sense that he is a part of the will of God, whether he likes it or not, and that he is dependent upon

Him for life, both here and in the hereafter. When one accepts Christ, then Christ dwells in him and therefore a part of the divine is in him and cannot therefore die, for God is eternal, *and if you are a part of Him, you inherit eternity.* We should not seek to alter the universe to shape our own hopes, dreams and desires, but we must reconcile ourselves to things as they are, or as they appear to be, and to what they will be, and maintain the utmost hope in everlasting life and in a heaven which has been promised to us, for this leads us to the greatest happiness we shall ever now and is the highest goal to which anyone can aspire—why ask for more?

Peter writes these words of assurance:

"By His great mercy we have been born anew to a living hope through the resurrection of Jesus Christ from the dead and to an inheritance which is imperishable, undefiled, and unfading, kept in heaven for you, who, by God's power, are guarded through faith for a salvation ready to be revealed in the last time. In this you rejoice, though now for a little while you may have to suffer various trials so that the genuineness of your faith, more precious than gold, which, through perishable, is tested by fire, may rebound to praise the glory and honor at the revelation of Jesus Christ. Without having seen Him you love Him; though you do not see Him now, you believe in Him and rejoice with unutterable and exalted joy. As the outcome of your faith you obtain the salvation of your souls. You have been born anew, not of perishable seed but of imperishable, through the living and abiding word of God."

If one believes in Jesus then he ought to also believe in heaven, for he shall never know the least disappointment. A hope in heaven, what more can the heart desire? What greater dream?

If one seeks after immortality then, after having made his peace with God, he should make himself the following promises, insofar as it pertains to his brethren:

"From this day forward all that I do will be because of love. I shall strive to cause no tear to be shed because of my desires, wishes and wants. No heart shall ache because of my vanity. My pride is of no import and if I could only but constran it so that the troubled heart of another shall find peace, then I would not care if what they do disagrees with my concept of right and wrong because I know that my own convictions might be faulty.

"In all that I do I shall strive to halt the flow of tears and bring happiness. If I could but soothe the troubled heart and bring peace to another, then, perhaps, mine own heart will heal.

"I shall shut my mouth if what I say causes another hurt or unhappiness. If by my words I bring hurt to another may I likewise know hurt to the degree that payment shall be in full.

"To be critical is to judge and my judgment may be faulty. To substitute my will for another's is an error, for I am self-willed and have not a contrite heart. If I bring an agony to any heart, young or old, or if I seek to cause youth to pass by the joys of youth and seek to subordinate youth's desires to mine, then I, an old man, sin, for youth will pass swift enough and shall know its own agonies—I need not add to them. *In love I shall seek to guide them, with the reins of love, and not with the whip or spur.* And should I fail, let it be me who weeps with a broken heart because of my failure and not becuase of what they do.''

XII

Good News

The following article recently appeared in one of our local newspapers:

"Why the Press does not come to its own defense is beyond my comprehension. The Press is being damned, badgered and dishonored by the lowly and by the great. If there is any group in America that most assuredly does not belong to the ' silent majority' it is the Press, yet it has been strangely silent in answering its critics.

The press ought to educate the public on what constitutes news. It should make the public aware of the fact that news is not the everyday event, the normal or commonplace, but *news is news simply because it is not normal or commonplace.*

For example, every Saturday I and all of my neighbors mow our lawns. That isn't news, but let one of us lose his fingers to the whirling blades and the whole neighbors comes alive with the news of the event and not one single teller thereof is criticized for relating the tragedy. But let the Press report the event and up goes the hue and cry: "Must you always report only the bad news and not the good news?"

It is the responsibility of newspapers to print all of the news whether it be good or bad, as it happens and as factually as possible. If the proportion of each appears to be out of balance, it is not the fault of the Press but the fault of humanity.

It also is the responsibility of the Press to advocate opinions based upon their editors' evaluation of the news through editorials, columnists and so forth. It is not their responsibility to do the thinking for the reader for it is he who must take all of the news, opinions and ideas presented by the Press, sift through them, evaluate them and then come to his own free, independent judgment and beliefs.

To take exception to an editorial or to a position taken by any given newspaper is one thing, but to criticize the Press, per se, is entirely another matter and the Press is under no obligation to print a contrary position or to print anything submitted to them which they consider to be in poor taste, ill-timmed, or not newsworthy.

"I submit that those who attack the free Press are not capable of unbiased opinion but objurgate it simply because the position taken therein contravenes their preconceived beliefs of what they consider contributes to the common good, or does not point to the end result which they themselves might think desirable, whether motivated by selfish interest or not.

Most people will accept that which agrees with what they already believe and reject that which disagrees with what they already believe. They are unable to cope with the irritation caused by anything that makes them doubt their beliefs. The art of believing is not enhanced by closing one's mind to what he considers to be evil and wrong, and opening it to what he considers to be good and right, for their conclusions might, lacking comparison, be faulty and in error.

The Press has, and always will influence people's opinions, thoughts and beliefs and if anyone lacks the conviction of his beliefs and if he fears the influence of the Press because it is disturbing to him, then he ought to take up the life of a hermit. As long as men communicate with each other they will always have an influence upon one another's thoughts and beliefs, whether agreeable or disagreeable.''

The same principles of evaluating news apply to the person evaluating the truth of the good news as set forth in the Scriptures. *It is not the responsibility of our ministers and our teachers to do our thinking for us*, but each of us must search the Scriptures, evaluate what is preached and taught, and then come to our own free, independent beliefs or not believe it. The decision to accept or reject it rests solely with each person; it is not compulsory, but in arriving at our decision one must always weight the possible alternatives, should he elect to reject the good news. It is a decision that should not be made lightly, for if we commit error the results might be irreversible.

1 Peter says to man: "Through Christ you have confidence in God, who raised Him from the dead and gave Him glory, so that your faith and hope are in God. Having purified your soul by your obedience to the truth for a sincere love of the brethren, love one another earnestly from the heart. You have been born anew, not of perishable seed but of imperishable, through the living and abiding word of God, for all flesh is like grass and all its glory like the flower of grass. The grass withers, and the flower falls, but the word of the Lord abides forever. That word is the good news which was preached to you."

The Bible is full of events and predictions about good news which is to come, and which has already happened. It was good news to the Jewish race when they were told that a Saviour would be born of the seed of Abraham, and that He would rule the world and that through Him there would be eternal life. It was good news to the Jews when they were told that their people had been selected to bear the messiah and that through them the word of God would be made known to all men, both Jew and the Gentile.

It was good news to the Jews when they were told that God had selected a parcel of ground and that He promised them the land for themselves and their generations to come.

It was good news to the Jewish people who were in slavery in Egypt when they were told that a leader would come and lead them out of captivity into the promised land. It was good news when they learned that Pharaoh had agreed to set them free and that Moses would lead them to the land that God had promised.

It was good news when the waiting world was told that the Saviour had been born in Bethlehem.

After Christ started His ministry, people spread the good news that He was coming to a village, or to a mountain, or that He would be at the site of a lake, and that He would teach them, and the news swept over the area. People would come for miles around to gather and to listen to His teachings.

When those who were cured from their diseases, their blindness, their lameness and their worries, how they must have hurried home to their loved ones to tell the good news that they were no longer blind, or deaf, or crippled, but that they were made whole by the saving grace of Jesus.

It was great news to the poor and to the downtrodden and to the hopeless when Christ gave them hope by saying:

"Blessed are the poor in spirit, blessd are those who mourn, blessed are the meek, blessed are those who hunger and thirst after righteousness, blessed are the merciful, blessed are the pure in heart, blessed are the peacemakers, blessed are those who are persecuted for righteousness' sake, blessed are you when men revile you and persecute you and utter all kinds of evil against you falsely on my account . . . for you are the light of the world."

What hope these struggling people must have gained from this good news. Christ gave good news to many, such as:

"Take heart, my son, your sins are forgiven."

"Take heart, daughter, your faith has made you well."

"Depart, for the girl is not dead but sleeping."

"Go and tell John what you hear and see, the blind receive their sight and the lame walk, lepers are cleansed and the deaf hear, and the dead are raised up, and the poor have good news preached to them, and blessed is he who takes no offense at me."

Christ proclaimed good news to the weary when He said:

"Come to me all who labor and are heavy laden and I will give you rest. Take my yoke upon you, and learn from me, for I am gentle and lowly in heart, and you will find rest for your souls. For my yoke is easy, and my burden is light."

"Lo, I am with you always, to the close of the age."

Then we have this great news:

"For God so loved the world that He gave His only Son that whosoever believes in Him should not perish but have eternal life. For God sent the Son into the world, not to condemn the world, but that the world might be saved through Him. He who believes in Him is not condemned, He who does not believe is condemned already, because he has not believed in the name of the only Son of God."

The great news that Christ proclaimed was, "I am the resurrection and the Life, he who believes in me, though he die, yet shall he live, and whosoever lives and believes in me shall never die."

It was great news to those who accepted what the disciples taught to the Jews and to the pagans, that through Christ there is hope for eternal life, that even though they break the law and stand condemned under it, they will, nevertheless, be saved from death through Christ. *What news for the hopeless when they learned that even though a man stands guilty and condemned under the law, under Christ they are acquitted and freed from the bonds of sin and death.*

It was great news to the Gentiles when they were told that the saving grace of Christ also was available to them and that they, too, had a hope of eternal life. When they learned that God, through Christ, had appointed a special apostle named Paul to carry to them the good news of salvation they rejoiced at receiving such good news.

Of course, the greatest news that reached those who loved Christ was the news that He had risen! These followers who felt the depths of despair at the news of His crucifixion were elated at the good news that He had risen from the dead. The disciples, upon learning the good news that He would appear to them, could hardly believe it. But He did, and they went across the land telling everyone they came in contact with the news of His resurrection. This news was so great that they gave their lives to spreading it, so that as many as possible would hear their good news.

The Bible also teaches the good news that this world of pain and sorrow will pass away, and a new world will come into being with Christ as King. That all of the sorrow, hurt and tears that we now shed will be washed away and there will be no tears, no sorrow, no death, for all these former things will pass away and we shall live with Him. Satan and evil will be bound for all eternity and man shall not know his works any more, but Christ shall receive into His own those who strive to follow after Him and who have learned to love. *This is the great news of the Bible.*

Many of us have lost sons, daughters, parents, wives and husbands, and our grief would be unbearable if we did not have a belief in the good news that they live, and we can believe this because we know that Christ lives. And we can believe this because He was seen by many after His resurrection. People who talked to Him, who touched Him, who saw Him. Not just one, or even two, but many. It has always been a mystery why when today when one or more people go before a court of law and testify that they saw someone commit an act that the courts and juries will believe them because of their testimony. Yet even though those who saw Christ after death testified to the event, there are *those who will not accept the same rules of evidence* as to His resurrection as they apply to the guilt or innocence of their fellow man. Matthew wrote of the risen Christ as follows: "Now the eleven disciples went to Galilee, to the mountain to which Jesus had directed them and when they saw Him they worshipped Him."

Mark wrote that He appeared first to Mary Magdalene, then to two disciples on the road, then to the twelve.

Luke wrote that He appeared to Mary, to Simon, and to the twelve after death.

Read John, commencing with the twentieth chapter and you have the most complete account of His resurrection and contact with the living after His death. All these writings are in testimony that He lives and this good news should give everyone who mourns comfort and assurance.

It may be news to you that the Bible only gives us a small account of the many things that Christ said and did, both during His life, and after His death. John aids in our understanding when he closes his book with the news that, "But there are also many other things which Jesus did; were every one of them to be written, I suppose that the world itself could not contain the books that would be written."

We have been speaking about news; well, just what is news?

Why did Christ become news wherever He went? The society in which we live has all of the human emotions: loves, hatreds, vanities, passions, ambitions, jealousies, loyalties and rivalries—and they exist in one form or another in the teeming life all around and about us. When these conflicting interests come into clash, creating an unusual effect and attracting the attention of all others within range of sight or hearing, that is news. The life of Christ came into direct conflict with the world and that is why He became news. He was different.

Whenever anything that is unusual happens which is contrary to the expectations of all who are involved in it or who have even casually noticed its normal operation, it becomes news. The life and teachings of Christ were unusual and contrary to the normal teachings of the rabbis and priests.

Whenever a blizzard, tornado, earthquake, tidal wave or cloud burst is a thing to which we are not accustomed, or do not anticipate, and when such happenings crash into our peaceful routines of existence, it becomes a phenomenon. All that is phenomenal is news. Christ was most assuredly a phenomenon, and His acceptance by millions, the way that He altered the course of mankind, all are phenomenal.

Anything that is unusual is news. The commonplace makes no news, but only the unusual. None can say that Christ was not an unusual man because He did unusual things, He said unusual things and His life, death and resurrection were unusual.

News is not always conflict, tragedy, or heartbreak. For example, an intellect rises above the commonplace and creates some marvel of science or philosophy. A thinker solves a problem that has vexed people for decades. These, too, are news, because once more they are different. Well, Christ most assuredly rose above the usual, the commonplace, and solved many of the mysteries of the world.

The first time anything is ever done it is news. Christ was the first risen and that was news!

Anything that has a spiritual quality and that transports millions of people into new heights of ecstasy is news. Christ has inspired more men to high ideals than any other religious figure, and that's news.

Any person who can shock the world out of its doldrums by bringing forth an earth-shattering revelation makes news. Christ surely shattered many of the old concepts of religious dogma.

The newsmen have a guideline that goes like this: "Boil it down to four lines—never more than four lines if a dog bites a man, but if a man bites a dog, write a column." If Christ had simply fallen into step with the rabbis, we would not have heard anything about Him, but He did not. He challenged their authority, and that was news.

It is news of the first magnitude when something or someone touches the pocketbook of other people, or if what they do touches their conscience or disturbs their habits of thought. Christ did just that in the doctrine of brotherly love, in causing people to examine their consciences, to search their hearts, and He disturbed their complacent habits of thought, and He still does so to this very day. That's news.

The greatest news stories are yet to come. News such as: The rapture of the church has taken place! The tribulation has begun! The seven bowls of judgment are being poured out! The seven trumpets are being sounded! The end is in sight! (What headlines these will make!) The Battle of Armageddon has begun! The back of evil has been broken and Satan has been cast into the pit! The millennium has taken place! Christ has taken His throne and rules the world! Satan has once more been loosed from his bounds and the world turns again to evil! The wrath of God has been poured out! Satan has been destroyed forever! The end has come, time has stopped, and eternity has begun! These will make great headlines in the newspapers when they occur. They will be frightening and hard to believe, and we will have to be strong in our faith when news of these events does occur. But the good news is that we, as Christians, will have no need to fear, if we stand steadfast in our belief in God and in the saving grace of His Son, and when the weeping and wailing and gnashing of teeth is heard we will be awfully glad that we know the good news.

There are many ways of learning about the good news of Christ. Through historical research, from reading the written record and from oral traditions, from sermons and Sunday school participation. All of these are, of course, only the tools for gaining knowledge about the new life that is offered through Christ. *But the news is "good" only when it brings us into fellowship with God, and with our fellow man, and enables us to realize the divine meaning of our lives.* It matters little if Luke or Paul or even Christ knew and spoke the word of God unless that word speaks to us in our own lives and we become aware of the living Christ and of the presence of God. It makes no difference if we simply shrug off the good news and go our way.

There is also the good news that Christ has not left us to our ends but continues to work with us through the Holy Spirit. The living reality of God's personal presence is what we mean by the term "Holy Spirit." Both Luke and Acts identify Christ closely with the Holy Spirit, personally present and active with His people. Our greatest news will be when we cry out to our loved ones, "He has chosen me!"

Luke wrote that Mary, the mother of Christ, was told by an angel, "The Holy Spirit will come upon you, and the power of the Most High will overshadow you, therefore the child to be born will be called holy, the Son of God."

Luke quoted John the Baptist as saying, "I baptize you with water, but He who is mightier than I is coming, the thong of whose sandals I am not worthy to untie, He will baptize you with the Holy Spirit and with fire."

Luke said, "Christ said, 'and everyone who speaks a word against the son of man will be forgiven, but he who blasphemes against the Holy Spirit will not be forgiven.' "

In Acts we read, "And they were all filled with the Holy Spirit and began to speak with other tongues, as the Spirit gave them utterance. And we are witnesses to these things, and so is the Holy Spirit whom God has given to those who obey Him." Speaking of the travels of Paul and Barnabas: "And they went through the region of Phrygia and Galatia, having been forbidden by the Holy Spirit to speak the word in Asia and when they had come opposite Mysia they attempted to go into Bithynia, but the Spirit of Jesus would not allow them."

Until we accept the good news about Jesus and allow the Holy Spirit to enter into our being, the news is of no import. Even the disciples who had lived with Jesus and knew Him were not fully qualified to witness for Him and Acts records that Christ said to them after He had risen, "He charged them not to depart from Jerusalem, but to wait for the promise of the Father, and He said, "You heard from me, for John baptized me with water, but before many days you shall be baptized with the Holy Spirit."

Paul wrote these words to the followers of Christ, and we should hope that the same words could be written to us: "For we are not, like so many, peddlers of God's word, but as men of sincerity, as commissioned by God, in the sight of God we speak in Christ . . . Do we need, as some do, letters of recommendation to you, or from you? You yourselves are our letter of recommendation, written on your hearts, to be known and read by all men, written not with ink but with the Spirit of the living God, not on tablets of stone but on tablets of human hearts."
Should we receive such a letter we would hasten to tell the good news to all we met.

John gives us this good news: "That which we have seen and heard we proclaim also to you . . . and this is the testimony, that God gave us eternal life, and this life is in His Son. He who has the Son has life, he who has not the Son has not life."

This is the good news, and we are extolled to report it to every man.

XIII

The Spirit

We are all familiar with the words, "The Father, the Son, and the Holy Ghost." The words "Ghost" and "Spirit" are synonymous and when used in a Biblical sense they have the same meaning.

The word "Holy" means anything entitled to worship or profound religious reverence because of its divine character or origin, or connection with God. Also specially recognized or declared sacred by religious use or authority, or consecrated. Also dedicated or devoted to the service of God, such as a church or religion or ritual as in holy water, holy church, or remember the Sabbath and keep it holy. It must have an air of saintliness or godliness and have an air of being pious or devout, such as a holy man. In many cases it has an air of mystery and awe. It must be deserving of being revered, and associated with it is an element of fear. For example, we speak of the Holy Bible and there are few of us who have the courage to deliberately deface it or to throw it into a trash heap as we would any other worn book *because we attach to it a feeling of reverence.* When one wear a gold cross suspended on a chain about the neck he feels attached to it, and when it is removed it is not tossed into the jewelry box as any other piece of jewelery, but is carefully lain in its place with tenderness. The same is true of rosary beads. *We treat them as holy objects because we associate them with God.*

The word "Spirit," or "Holy Ghost," is derived from the principle that the body and the spirit are separate, the incorporeal being as opposed to matter. It is that which is present in life, but separate from the body, or absent at death, as stated in Ecclesiastes, "And the spirit shall return unto God who gave it." It also means the soul, or the seat of thought and feeling dealing especially with the moral or religious nature of man. It is associated with the supernatural, as "God is a spirit." It is also associated with the inner feelings, the inner self; as Timothy said, "The Lord Jesus Christ be with thy spirit." It is referred to as the seat of all feelings or sentiments.

When we use the words "Holy Spirit" we are thinking of the Spirit of God which inspires us and influences our actions and thoughts. In Numbers

75

we read, "When the spirit rested upon them, they prophesied"; and in Isaiah, "Until the spirit be poured upon us from on high." It means an inner influence as an agency working in the hearts of men. And in Romans, "He that raised up Christ from the dead shall also quicken your mortal bodies by His spirit that dwelleth in you."

What is the nature of the Holy Spirit? In John we read, "The wind blows where it wills, and you hear the sound of it, but you do not know whence it comes or whither it goes, so it is with everyone who is born of the spirit." Yet we are able to possess it. *Every man is basically a product of what he chooses to identify with.* If he identifies with power, he is a tyrant; if with possessions, a materialist; if with appearance, an egotist; and with the Holy Spirit, a Christian. The mark of the Christian is the individual who is in possession of the Spirit but he can possess it only when it is given to him by God when the Spirit rests upon him.

In Acts, Peter, standing with the eleven, lifted up his voice and addressed them: "Men of Judea and all who dwell in Jerusalem, this be known to you, and give ear to my words . . . this is what was spoken by the prophet Joel, 'And in the last days it shall be, God declares, that I will pour out my Spirit upon all flesh, and your sons and your daughters shall prophesy, and your young men shall see visions, and your old men shall dream dreams, yea, and on my menservants and my maidservants in those days I will show wonders in the heaven above and signs on the earth beneath. Blood and fire, and vapor or smoke, the sun shall be turned into darkness and the moon into blood before the day of the Lord comes, the great and manifest day. And it shall be that whoever calls on the name of the Lord shall be saved.' "

The Spirit of God was with the world from the beginning, we read in Genesis: "And the earth was without form, and void, and darkness was upon the face of the deep, and the Spirit of God moved upon the face of the waters." The Holy Spirit has endowed faithful men with wisdom and knowledge through out all of man's life. "And Pharaoh said unto his servants, 'Can we find such a one as this is, a man in whom the Spirit of God is?' And Pharaoh said unto Joseph, 'For as much as God hath shewed thee all this, there is none so discreet and wise as thou art.' " And in Deuteronomy we read: "And Joshua the son of Nun was full of the spirit of wisdom for Moses had laid his hands upon him, and the Children of Israel hearkened unto him, and did as the Lord commanded Moses." The Holy spirit has worked in the affairs of men from the beginning and is working today. When one has an awareness that God works through a mysterious but discernible way that is not physical but spiritual, then an understanding of what is meant by the Holy Ghost suddenly clarifies itself. This understanding becomes the confirming principle marking members of the true church. His presence and the awareness of His presence makes the essential difference between belief and faith. Without an awareness of the influence of the Holy Spirit no person is truly a part of the Body of Christ, nor can he become a stone set into the temple of God.

It was because the Apostles had experienced the presence of the Holy Spirit in their own lives that they could communicate convincingly the power of Christ and cut through divisions and traditions of the world and then transform the lives of men. Wherever they went, the blaze of faith radiated because they knew what they were to do, being informed by the Holy Spirit. They became witnessees to the whole world and prepared others to receive the Spirit's confirmation of the presence of God in their lives.

Some of the last words recorded what Jesus said on the earth were reported by Matthew: "All authority in heaven and on earth has been given to me. Go therefore and make disciples of all nations, baptizing them in the name of the Father and of the Son and of the Holy Spirit, teaching them to observe all that I have commanded you, and lo, I am with you always, to the close of the age." St. Luke records that He forbade them to go until they had received the Spirit. Christ told them: "Thus it is written, that the Christ should suffer and on the third day rise from the dead, and that repentence and forgiveness of sins should be preached in his name to all nations, beginning from Jerusalem. You are witnesses of these things, and behold, I send the promise of my Father upon you, but stay in the city until you are clothed with power from on high." And when the Holy Spirit descended upon them they became of one accord and declared: "There is one body and one Spirit, one Lord, one Faith, one baptism. One God and Father of all, who is above all, and through all and in you all. But unto every one of us is given grace according to the measure of the gift of Christ."

In the Old Testament the purpose of the Holy Spirit was to call men to God, to give them wisdom and leadership and guidance, and to work in the hearts of men so that they might be brought into fellowship with God. *In the New Testament the primary work of the Holy Spirit is to enable men to recognize the person of Jesus Christ.* It is through the Holy Spirit that Christ becomes a living person, and not just a memory. You will recall that after Peter felt the wind of the Spirit his first act was to testify to the reality of the Messiah. Because of the unity of the divine nature of God, the presence of the Spirit carries with it the whole nature of God and the whole person of Christ. Whenever the Spirit falls upon an individual, the result is an actual, immediate fellowship with the total nature of God in Christ. The awareness of His presence serves to cause our worship to be not empty repetition but makes us come alive with an awareness of the divine reality. It brings us fully alive and we cast off our former selves and we can do nothing other than good works, not for reward, but for love. Galatians teaches, "For, Brethren, ye have been called unto liberty, only use not liberty for an occasion to the flesh, but by love serve one another. For all the law is fulfilled in one word, even in this: Thou shalt love thy neighbor as thyself. But if ye bite and devour one another, take heed that ye be not consumed by another. This I say then, walk in the Spirit, and ye shall not fulfill the lust of the flesh. For the flesh lusteth against the Spirit, and the Spirit against the flesh. And these are contrary one to the other, so that ye cannot do the things that you would. But if ye be led of the Spirit, ye are not under the law. Now the *works of the flesh* are manifest, which are these, adultery, fornication, uncleanness, idolatry, witchcraft, hatred, wrath, strife, seditions, heresies, envy, murder, drunkenness, revellings and such like. Of the which I tell you before, as I have also told you in time past, that they which do such things shall not inherit the kingdom of God.

"But the *fruits of the Spirit* are love, joy, peace, long-suffering, gentleness, goodness, faith, meekness, temperance, against such there is no law. And they that are Christ's have crucified the flesh with the affections and lusts. If we live in the Spirit, let us also walk in the Spirit."

Paul speaks in Romans: "The Spirit himself bearing witness with our spirit that we are children of God." These are words of assurance. Without them the Christian is forever uncertain of his own relationship with God. With this assurance he is filled with confidence, and therefore, with a feeling of power, of freedom. And we can be assured that the Holy Ghost will descend upon the children of God and those who have faith in Christ because he said: "But the comfortor, which is the Holy Ghost, whom the father will send in my name, he shall teach you all things and bring all things to your remembrance, whatsoever I have said unto you. Peace I leave with you, not as the world giveth, give I unto you. Let not your hearts be troubled, neither let it be afraid."

We should all be moved by the great concern that Christ had that men should not fear and be afraid. He must have recognized what a terrible thing fear is. Fear of Life, fear of death, fear that death is the end, fear during war, fear of the dark, fear of being alone, fear that loved ones will die, fear is everywhere and He said over and over, Fear not, be not fearful, have no fear, do not be afraid. So concerned is God that men not fear that Christ said that even when He is gone the Comfortor will be with us so that we will not be left alone. He assured us over and over that God, or He, or the Spirit of God would be with us always, until the end of time. We are never alone and this is why the Psalmist wrote, "Yea, tho I walk through the valley of the shadow of death, I shall fear no evil for thou art with me."

Every day we hear the politicians, the experts, and the brainchilds expound upon the ills of the world and how they propose to correct them. *They have pat answers for all our problems.* They crank up their computers and grind out solutions to all our ills. In support of their theories they loot, burn and pillage. They write their love ballads, and paste their flowers upon billboards and walls and upon their automobiles. Page after page of our magazines and newspapers are full of the writings of the people who will tell us what we should do and how we shall cure our ills. *Our bookshelves are loaded with their advice and counsel.* Yet the world grows worse and evil abounds. But men will find no peace nor freedom from fear until they become aware of the presence of the Spirit of God among the people. No human program can replace it nor substitute for it. The problems of the world will not yield to human ideas or methods but will fade only when men feel the presence of the Spirit of God. *God is not dead, it is the hearts of men that are dead to the Spirit of God.* You can feel his Spirit everywhere, at this moment, yet men say He is dead and they go about their business of trying to solve problems too complex for the human mind to grasp, let alone solve, and they refuse to listen to the Spirit of God.

The complex problems that we face today must be solved within the context and meaning of biblical doctrine and we must call upon the Holy Spirit to guide us and to counsel us. Failure to do so will result in the utter destruction of life as we now know it. Think not? Consider the atom bomb, the world power struggles, the corruption and evil that swirl around us touching us each day of our lives. *We have tried it alone and we have failed.* In the beginning God was with man but man would not listen. Later His Son Christ was with us and once more we would not listen, then Christ said that His Father would send the Comforter but, again, we will not listen and doomsday approaches.

I have just completed reading the projections into the years 1990 and 2000 made by some of the most knowledgeable men in the world, called the Rome Club, by federal agencies, by men in industry. These reports tell of over population, food shortages, energy shortages, housing shortages, economic woes. We will be running out of oil and gas and water and space, and all of the necessities of life. These are in-depth studies and are not the mere cries of doom by the radicals but studies of men who have devoted their lives to the subject.

These same studies come up with possible solutions and recommendations, but these are in for much delay because we will be unable to act in time to ward off the shortages because of greed and strife and personal gain. These traits will block all attempts to timely solve our problems.

The only problem with these studies and predictions of the end of the world is that *it always assumes that it is in the hands of man and not in the hands of God* and we go our merry way listening to men who claim to have answers to all problems and not to the wisdom of God. There are answers to our problems, but they are costly and time-consuming. But if men would seek the truth and the wisdom of God, they could work out the problems. God is called the Spirit of Truth in the Bible, but we reject these truths because we lack the intelligence to recognize them, or to listen to them and act accordingly.

In the face of the dilemmas that we face, men still reject God and pin their hopes and energies on human progress and on the "here and now" values rather than upon the eternal. This results, in part, *because man will not admit the sovereignty of God.* It is His world, it is in His hands, and He will control its destiny and will bring it to an end in His own time, but men deny this and say that the destiny of the world is in the hands of men.

Let us assume that men do and will control the destiny of the world and pin our hopes on human progress and assume that science can solve all our physical problems and overcome nature. But even if this planet could survive for another million years, or even 10 million years, *at some point in time it would come to an end.* Perhaps by the sun burning out, or because of a collision with another star, or we simply use up all of our resources; at some point it will come to an end. What then? Shall we then point with pride to human progress? What then will be the reward, and for whom? What a sorry end for humanity, for all his struggles were for naught. Well, *human life simply cannot pin its hopes upon human progress, but must look to something more than just living out whatever time is allotted to this planet and then sans end.* To what shall we look? Why, of course, to the promises of God, to life, to a place described in the Book of Revelation where God shall "wipe away all tears from their eyes, and there shall be no more death, neither sorrow, nor crying , neither shall there be any more pain, for the former things are passed away." This is the story that we must tell, this is where we must strive to lead our fellow men, this is our charge and if we fail then one day all humanity will come tumbling down and Christ will have died for nothing. And it is we who must shoulder the blame because of our silence. We have been charged to tell of Christ to all the world and the sooner we get about our business, as Christ went about His Father's business, the sooner that all mankaind will first see a ray of hope, and then a blazing light of understanding as they bask in the light of the word.

Do not fear that you do not have the power to fulfill your charge, for if you truly seek to serve God then it is written in Acts, "you shall receive power when the Holy Spirit has come upon you, and you shall be my witness in Jerusalem and in all Judea and Samaria and to the end of the Earth."

The Holy Spirit will descend upon all those who truly believe in the statement that Christ is the Son of God. If you do not believe this then your words are dust and your faith a fraud!

XIV

The Search

We have all heard about the search for the Holy Grail. It is supposed to be the cup used by Christ at the Last Supper and which thereafter became the object of knightly quest. If any knight had ever succeeded and had found the Holy Grail, the search would have ended then and there. No longer would knights have ridden through strange lands in search of that which had already been found.

Men through the ages have been and are still engaged in another holy quest and that is a search for God. It has been a restless search engaged in by both the lowly and the high, the primitive and civilized man, the rich and the poor—all are engaged in this ceaseless quest.

Many men embark upon the search simply because they cannot believe, they dedicate their lives to the search, only to fail and to sink back into oblivion and die in their unbelief. Others find Him and nothing can cause them to believe that they have not. Those who believe try to show those who do not believe how to find Him, but in many cases are unable to do so because they cannot find willing ears, they will not hear. For those who do find Him, the search is over and, as in the case of the Holy Grail, had it been found, the search ended. They are content to live and to bask in the light of the love of God.

But here is a mystery, for many profess that they have found Him, that they believe, *yet they continue to search as if some haunting doubt was agonizing their souls*. They embark upon studies of world religions, they attend to the doctrines of mystics and soothsayers. They entertain reincarnation, spiritualism, and witchcraft—yet all the while professing that they have found God. Is it not strange that having found God they continue to search? Would it not have been strange, had the Holy Grail ever been found, that knights would still have ridden out to face unknown dangers in search of that which was no longer lost? Challenge those who profess that they have found God and yet search, *and they respond that all they seek is to expand their knowledge of God*. Yet, they would expound upon their new-found knowledge as though they had found some new truth and, in many cases, a new God, often a fraudulent God, one more compatible with their own desires of how they think life ought to be. Their veracity is subject to question, for although it is true that if one embarks upon the quest to find God then he should explore and pursue all sources of knowledge, and if blessed with sufficient courage to follow that quest no matter where it might lead, then once they find Him they should search no more, for continued search would only be futile and pathetic and it belies the profession of faith they make. One does not need to continue to search for that which has been found, for that which is no longer lost.

Those who find Him early in life are indeed most fortunate, for they need never embark upon the quest; they simply say, "Be still, my heart, the Lord speaketh." If one truly finds God he is restless no more, he searches no longer, he delights in the knowledge that he has found that which he has sought and in the knowledge that the gates of hell cannot prevail against his conviction, belief, and trust.

The following remarks are directed primarily to those who may not have found Him and to those who say that they have, but have not, in the hope that some will see the paths that led to truth and to God, paths which are both dependable and trustworthy.

Who is this God that we seek?

We could go into high-sounding phrases about His being the creator of all things, a God of love, a God of justice, all-wise, all-powerful, kind, benevolent, being disposed to the happiness of His subjects. We could spend endless hours speculating and expounding upon the many beliefs that we hold. It has been said that no two people hold to the same beliefs, either within a single denomination or between denominations, or between brother and brother, brother and sister, father and mother, or sons and daughters. All come to their independent beliefs and hold to them, denying all that disagrees with what they already believe and accepting that which agrees with what they already believe. If you do not believe this, engage any person you know in a religious discussion and you will find disagreement within five minutes, and each will state differently who God is and what He is like.

But who does God say he is? He speaks of Himself in the first four commandments and of His desire.

"*I am the Lord thy God* which have brought thee out of the land of Egypt, out of the house of bondage. Thou shalt have no other Gods before me."

That is all! "I am the Lord thy God." No elaborate attempt to explain His origin, no explanation about how and why he created the unvierse. He simply stated, "I am the Lord thy God." *This apparently is all that He believes we need to know, that He is the Lord our God.* In return for His being our God, all He asks is total dedication. He simply states, "Thou shall have no other Gods before me." No other thing, not money, power, influence, or fame, no false Gods, nothing but that we merely accept the words, "I am the Lord thy God." There is no clearer way to express it! How ridiculously simple! How uncomplicated! "I am the Lord thy God!!"

Then he proceeds: "Thou shall not make unto thee any graven image, or any likeness of anything that is in heaven above or that is in the earth beneath or that is in the water under the earth." He is telling us here that He is sovereign, that He and He alone is God and that we are not to bow down before any other God. Well, why should we? If we believe that *God is God*, then no other god can or should receive our homage. The request is so reasonable that it is self-evident.

"Thou shalt not take the name of the Lord thy God in vain." Here He demands reverence and honor, love and respect. This is not much to ask. Do we not ourselves ask the same from our own children? It is a perfectly simple request and it is not in the least difficult to understand, nor should it be questioned by any true believer.

"Remember the sabbath day and keep it holy." Even God rested on the seventh day. It is a day set aside for rest and to recuperate from the strains of life and living in this world. It is a day for us to renew our strength, cleanse our minds, and rest our bodies. It is a day to pause and remember Him, just one day a week; this is not much to ask. This commandment is not solely for His benefit, but is also directed to us in our own interest and for our own benefit.

The foregoing is what He says of Himself and of our relationship with Him, that is, man to God. *It contains all that He demands.* All that we read and hear about man to God can be related to these first four commandments. Thus we do not find a despotic God, for His demands are few, and to the believer they create no insurmountable obstacles. In the application of our relationship with him, when related to the commandments, it requires only a small amount of understanding and should stir within us a feeling that we should have done all these things even if He had not asked it of us, for they are the normal demands of love.

The balance of the Ten Commandments deal with man's relationship with man.

How and where do we learn more about this God?

Well, we can read the great works of the theologians, but it is the Bible that forms the primary source for our Christian belief and it supplies the information concerning our God. But here most men fail in their search for God *because most men seek to know more about the Bible instead of seeking knowledge about God through the Scriptures*, and that is the underlying message of the Bible. We do not need to defend the Scriptures to any man, but we do need to make daily use of them. *The Bible suffers more from disuse than from abuse and attack.* How can we prove the inspiration of the Bible to those who doubt? We cannot, because this is a faith judgment. The apostles did not argue the point, they witnessed to their own experiences in the Scriptures. Paul wrote in 1 Corinthians, "Now we have received not the spirit of the world, but the spirit which is from God, that we might understand the gifts bestowed on us by God. And we impart this in words not taught by human wisdom but taught by the spirit, interpreting spiritual truths to those who possess the Spirit."

Our faith is not founded on a printed book, but on a living Person in the man Jesus Christ; However, the only place we have a firsthand account of that Person and His teachings is in the New Testament. It is also the only authority that we as Christians have concerning the existence of God and of His instructions to mankind. It is the Christian's chief source of knowledge concerning the being, character, and will of God. It is our record of God's revelation of Himself to men, and this can come only from reading it and not by just glancing through it.

Well, how does one know when he has found God? How can one be sure?

A boy and a girl meet, they fall in love. If you ask them how they know they are in love, you will receive all kinds of romantic answers. But press the question and the final answer that you will recieve is, "I know I am." If you ask, "How do you know you are?," their reply comes back, "I cannot explain it, I just know that I am." All attempts to tell them they are just infatuated with each other fail. If you try to tell them that all they have is a physical attraction for each other, they will deny it. If you try to discourage marriage by reasons of economics, education, compatibility, status and social differences, your pleas, logic, and arguments fall upon deaf ears. *They are in love.* They know they are in love. And nothing you can say can possibly change their conviction or make them believe otherwise. *They are in love.* They have faith in that love and to that end are willing to risk their lives in dedication to each other and stand ready to endure any sacrifice required to assure that they will be together until death do them part.

But when the hardships of life descend upon them in full fury, far too many times they fall away and love dies and they go their separate ways. Nevertheless, when they were in love, all attempts to tell them otherwise failed because they believed their love to be true.

So it is with one who truly finds God. He knows that he has found Him and all attempts to convince him otherwise are doomed to failure. The philosophers have tried to do so with logic so strong that it is difficult to refute their arguments. But they fail and those who know that they have found God stand steadfast in the face of all their arguments. Governments have tried to stamp out their belief. They have killed them, tortured them, banned them from society, but they will not deny their faith or their belief that they have found God; and, as in the case of lovers, no amount of logic, reasoning, or oppression by those who oppose their beliefs can have any effect whatsoever upon the true believer.

Ask him how he knows that there is a God and the response is, "I know." But ak him how he knows and the reply comes back, "I do not know why I believe it, I only know that I do." Press him for his proof and the answer is, "I cannot prove it but I know that I have found Him and I will follow Him no matter where He leads. *I have found Him.* I am sure of it. My quest is over and I will defend my right to believe in Him against all trials and against all comers."

Knowledge that one has found God rests ultimately in faith, and anyone who has a deep conviction and faith need never ask, "how can I find God?" because he knows that he has already found Him, or is convinced that he has, and no man thereafter has the right to try to convince him otherwise. It is his perfect right, and error is committed only by those who seek to destroy it, not by the believer.

One cannot prove the existence of God by comparison to things real. All methods of proving a theory, an idea, or supposition by scientific inquiry fail. He cannot be proved by any of our senses such as sight, sound, touch, or smell. One cannot produce a single shred of tangible evidence that He, in fact, exists, and even if one points to things real, the skeptic will retort that all things just happened by spontaneous reaction and are not as the result of any creative power. *Yet in the face of all this, when one does find God, there remains no doubt; his conviction is absolute.* We have known true believers who have suffered all manner of hardships, who have lost loved ones, lost their homes in disasters, their health, wealth, and all that they possess, and yet stand steadfast, because they know. People caught up in great natural disasters, who have witnessed friends and relatives being killed all about them and they, themselves, hurt and crippled, still stand steadfast to their belief in God. Great wars have done untold damage, destroyed civilizations, ravaged the land, terror and torture being the order of the day, yet those who believe in God, who know that He exists, do not waver in their belief that they have found Him.

Whole nations of people pray to Him. Millions bow down before Him each day. *When so many have prayed throughout the ages, one needs to pause and ask himself how he, standing alone, can question the validity of a claim made by so many millions that they have found God.* It is an audacious position for one to take.

One philosopher wrote, "The fact that millions of people throughout the ages have held to an erroneous belief does not prove it to be true, for all men of all ages can be wrong." But our response to him should be that all men of all ages can be right, and our claim has as much validity as does his, the difference being that he does not know for certain what he says, while we do, because we know for certain that there is a God. How do we know? *Because we have found Him.* Our quest is over and no man shall ever make us believe otherwise.

Have you ever wondered why there are so many ideas of what God is like? And why is it that whenever you become engaged in a discussion with another person about Him that almost at once you find yourself involved in difference of opinion? Sometimes these differences are so great that they result in outright argument and flares of temper, and, in some cases, in loss of friendship.

It is impossible to pray or to believe in nothing, so the mind must reduce any God or deity that is worshipped to a mental image or form, one to whom one can speak and communicate. The pagan and primitive built idols and totem poles and animal forms and worshipped them as gods. These were something tangible, something one could feel and touch which added an element of reality to belief. Throwbacks to the primitive still exist in the modern church in the form of the cross, statues of the Virgin Mary, beads, holy objects, etc. These constitute a physical bind between the worshipper and God.

Once having created our image of God in our own mind, we must then reduce Him to a personality. He must have certain traits that are compatible with what we believe a God should feel, how He should act, what His will should be, and what His designs are. *The closer we build our mental God to our own character and beliefs, the easier it is to worship Him.* We come to believe that what we find offensive must likewise be offensive to Him. What we believe to be good and evil, He must also believe to be good and evil. Many of us come to believe that God should be like us and not us like God, because we become convinced or our own greatness and, therefore, believe that surely God must likewise be as good as are we. We like the personal association with such a God who is so easy to follow and to understand. We like our mental God because He gives us no problems and we are comfortable in our belief. Some even go so far as to believe that He is some kind of cosmic servant available to us upon beck and call.

Now, someone else has different ideas and beliefs and he has created in his mind a picture of his God and has assigned to Him personality traits which are compatible to his own but which differ from ours; thus, when a discussion is had and something said which disagrees with our mental picture of God, this creates irritation. It disturbs us because our mental God has come under attack, so we try to show the other person *that his God is false while ours is true.* Arguments ensue or, in the least, disagreements. It makes us uncomfortable. We are happy with our mental God and we do not want our beliefs upset, so we rejected what the other party is saying.

With so many people having so many different images of what God should be like, then how can we truly know what He is really like, His true traits, His true personality, His true will and design? The only record we Christians have which contains answer to these questions is contained in the Scriptures. "Seek and ye shall find." But, having found that which you seek, search no more for you have already found the greatest of all human wisdoms!

XV

Prayer

In almost every case, when someone says that God answered his prayers, it is possible to find logical reasons why it came about. And, by the way, this is one of the most amazing things about prayers. After most prayers have been answered, the answers were so readily available as to make one wonder why he did not see the answer in the first place and merely act upon the situation without resorting to prayer. When one uses his God-given talents then he knows that God does answer prayers.

Most people form the idea that to pray is to ask God for some favor, benefit or help, either spiritual or material, or both. However, prayer can also be the giving of adoration, or the act of confession or thanksgiving, or in some cases simply communicating with God. Prayer can be a deep personal thing which can move one into feelings of ecstasy and can have powerful uplifting effects upon one's emotions. Or it can merely be something routine, such as the spinning of a Tibetan prayer wheel, or the pulling of a card from a box of prayers and reading it, or flicking the pages of a prayer book to a given day and reading the printed prayer.

Before one can effectively pray, he must reduce the power to whom he is praying to a form or deity and reduce it to a being with a personality capable of responding very much as does the prayer. It is quite impossible to pray to a shapeless, meaningless power, so the power must generally be reduced to a mental conception of a form or being, having the ability to communicate, to listen, to hear, to feel and to respond, otherwise the act of prayer is nothing more than a ritual.

Many times we feel that our prayers are not heard and that, if heard, they were not answered, which really means that we feel that we did not get what we asked for. *We should be thankful that God does not answer all prayers exactly as asked because if He did, we might well wish that He had not.* Take, for example, the Lord's Prayer, where we say, "Forgive us this day our trespasses, as we forgive those who trespass against us." If He were to respond and forgive us as we forgive those who trespass against us, I fear that we would all be in deep trouble. Likewise there are many things that we ask for that simply are not to our benefit and it takes a strong person of faith to believe this when he has offered up a sincere prayer only to find it unanswered. We might even become embittered and feel that God has abandoned us to our fate and feel that if He heard He ought to have answered our prayer. But, of course, this is an assumption, because we really do not know if He ought to have or not. We say and feel that He should have, but this may be false, unless we are willing to take the position that we know what is best for us while God does not.

Of course, one's attitude toward prayer is all-important because many times we pray for things that we ourselves should and can handle. There is a story about a man who lost his job and came home and knelt down by his bedside and prayed, "Oh God, my children are hungry, my wife is hungry, we need food. Please send us a chicken." The following day no chicken appeared and the man once more knelt down and prayed the same prayer. Once more the chicken did not appear. On the third day he again knelt down to pray and while he was praying his wife came in and kicked him. The man arose, anger in his eyes, and asked, "Woman, what is wrong with you? Here I am praying to God that He will send us a chicken, and you come in and kick me." She replied, "Husband, when you kneel down to pray, do not ask God to send you a chicken, but ask God to give you the ambition, the know-how, and the willpower to go out and get a job to earn sufficient money to buy a chicken." The following day they had a chicken to eat. Too many times we pray the wrong way. We want things but do not want to exert any effort on our own part to get the things we want.

Many times the things we pray for the hardest are right within our reach but we fail to recognize it. It may be under our very noses but still we just wail for God to give us this or that. It is like the story of a scientist who placed a large bass in a fish tank and did not feed it for several days until it had become a mighty hungry bass. Then one day he placed a piece of glass in the tank and divided the tank into two parts. He then placed a minnow on the opposite side of the glass divider and at once the bass made a mighty lunge at that minnow but banged his nose on the glass. He backed up and banged it again and again. Soon his nose was split and swollen and he began to strike with less and less power. Finally he nudged the glass, and at last gave up trying at all. The scientist then removed the glass divider and the minnow swam all around that bass but the bass knew that he could not eat that minnow, so it starved to death.

Many of us are very much like that bass. Answers to our problems are all around us. Ways of getting what we want are available to us. Ways of turning sorrow to happiness, tears to smiles, hate to love, war to peace, and on and on are available to us but we become so certain that we cannot help ourselves that we simply let our soul die and wither away, all the time beseeching God to do for us what we ourselves could do. We can fulfill many of our desires, hopes, dreams and longings if we would but exert a little effort and do it.

You can be assured that willy-nilly praying will avail you nothing, not even spiritual uplift, if you do not use the God-given powers and abilities that have been allotted to you. When a child learns to walk, you do not walk for him, he walks alone and grows in confidence. But if we were to walk for the child, or if God were to walk for us, neither would grow and develop self-assurance. It is what one accomplishes that gives him the greatest pride using his God-given talents, and it is then that we feel the greatest gratification to God and we should turn our faces toward heaven and give thanks that He let us work it out, thereby building strength, not dependency; courage, not cowardice; endurance, not weakness; and, above all self-esteem.

There are those who feel that prayer is unnecessary because God already knows our needs. Well, whoever said that the only time we are to pray is when we need something? Those who say that prayer is foolish base their arguments on the fact that God is omnipotent, meaning that He is unlimited in power, ability, and authority, and that He is almighty and can therefore provide us with our every whim and need. But, the trouble here is that to do so would destroy us. Scientists will tell you that if we feed birds and animals all they need, provide them with all the shelter, all the food and other wants, that they soon become so dependent on man's help that they can no longer survive in their natural habitats. *So it would be with man.* He would become so dependent on God that he could not survive in the world, and that is where he was designed to live.

The same people state that He is likewise omniscient, meaning that He has universal knowledge and is infinitely wise and therefore most assuredly knows what is best for us and should therefore provide the best for us. Well, what makes us think that He has not? The problem is that we do not avail ourselves of the best, but settle for second best, for the mediocre. He has given to man all of the tools he needs to love others, to find happiness, to live with a free spirit, to seek after nobility, to rise to heights not yet attained by man. All material and spiritual needs have been provided. Who is to blame if we do not use them for the purposes that they were intended—God or Man?

Their arguments continue. He is also omnipresent, meaning that He is present everywhere at once and therefore most assuredly know our needs and desires and that He could not claim that He did not knows what we want or need. It is agreed that He is omnipresent and can therefore witness how we do not use his gifts in the right manner and how He must shake His head and wonder, "What is the matter? Are they blind? What they ask for has been provided. It is at their fingertips. It is right before them. Why do they ask me for that which I have already given to them?" The greatest sorrow that we cause God is our refusal to use that which has been provided for our use and then wail for His help. It must be a frustration to Him and why He does not angrily cry out, "Use the things that I have provided—I have given you what ye seek, use it," is a mystery.

And then comes their last argument regarding the uselessness of prayer, for they say that God is benevolent and is therefore disposed to promote the prosperity and happiness of His subjects, that He is kind and charitable and therefore should remove from the world all that is hurtful to man. *The most hurtful things to man are the things that man does to himself.* We confuse the issue, for we compare hurts to the flesh with hurts of the spirit. The flesh is of this world and not of God. The spirit is of God and is of concern to Him. The mother does not look to the embryo but to the child. The good mother does all that she can to protect the growing child in the womb with the view of having a fine baby. If outside influences occur or if her conduct destroy the embryo, then the child is lost to her. But if she truly wants a child she will try again until at last one is born unto her. So it is with God, some souls are destroyed by yielding to outside influences or merely by destroy themselves. Other souls grow in love and into full bloom and it is they who belong to God. It is they who will dwell in the house of God.

God will give the flesh life but it is up to the flesh to give life to the spirit. If it does otherwise, the spirit will die unto God. We abort our mission in life if we refuse to use our God-given talents, fail to utilize the material things provided in a wise and prudent manner, and then turn in prayer to God and ask for the things that we ourselves already have but will not use. Is it any wonder that many feel that their prayers are not answered?

Matthew states: "Ask and it will be given to you." (*Just ask, look about and take it. It is there for your taking*); "Seek and you shall find." (*Open your eyes, it is right before you. You can find it.*); "Knock and it will be opened to you." (*If you cannot find it, knock. He will take you by the arm and point it out to you.*) "For everyone who asks receives, and he who seeks finds, and to him who knocks it will be opened." (*Ask, seek, knock and you will see His gifts all about you.*) "Or what man of you, if his son asks him for a loaf, will give him a stone, or if he asks for a fish, will give him a serpent. If you, then, who are evil, know how to give good gifts to your children, how much more will your father who is in heaven give good things to those who ask him?" (*Everything that the heart can desire has been provided.*) "So do whatever you wish that men would do to you, so do to them, for this is the law and the prophets." (*Hope, love and charity towards your fellow man will bring greater happiness than any other of the gifts of God. If we refuse to use them, these gifts that we already have, how can we justify praying for happiness?*)

Romans records: "Likewise, the Spirit helps us in our weakness, for we do not know how to pray as we ought, but the Spirit himself intercedes for us with sighs too deep for words."

Matthew reported that Christ said, "And in praying do not heap up empty phrases as the gentiles do, for they think that they will be heard for their many words. Do not be like them, for your Father knows what you need before you ask Him." God *knows* our needs before we ask. This is why

He has provided everything that we will need. But we will not correctly use what has been provided. Of the needs of the spirit every man has been provided for equally. For the needs of the flesh there is inequality. Why? Because God provided unequally? No, it is because man refuses to share the needs of the flesh equally among his fellow men, and uses greed, hate, lust for power and all the rest to grab for himself all that he can at the expense of his weaker brethren. No man would need to pray to God for worldly needs, needs of the flesh, if others did not take more than their share. There is enough for all. None would go wanting if only man would love his neighbor as himself. No poverty, no starvation, no war, no murder, and on and on if man would but share the things that his brethren pray for.

Does God answer our prayers? Of course He does! Whenever we earnestly pray for something, and if we simply will not see that the things we pray for are attainable, and if we will not use our God-given talents, then you may be sure that he does heave a great sigh too deep for words and takes us by the hand and says: "There is what you prayed for. It was there all the time. Take it."

I remember years ago when I was teaching a group of young teenagers about prayer and one small boy rose and said that he had prayed for a bicycle and had never gotten it and asked why God had not answered his prayer. He said that his father had assured him that God always answers prayers, and he had prayed, but he did not get a bicycle. I asked him what he had done to get one besides merely asking God to provide him with one. I asked him if he offered to mow lawns in his neighborhood, to do odd jobs, to save his allowance to accumulate enough money to buy a bicycle. *Three months later that boy was riding around on a brand spanking new bicycle!* He used his God-given talents and his prayers were answered.

Does God ever answer prayers for things over which man can exercise no control? Again, the answer is yes. Always? No. Why? Because we do not know the divine will of God. Whenever our will contravenes God's will, you can be certain that God's desires will be fulfilled for some good purpose, which we cannot always understand. There is no doubt concerning the justness of God. How can we be so dogmatic that He does hear and answer prayers about things over which we can exercise no control? Well, basically because of past experiences that have occurred in our own lives.

Some prayers are faith-destroying, for we pray against things that we ourselves could prevent, and when our prayers are not answered we begin to question our belief in prayer. Mass praying probably contributes more to his than does individual prayers. Some examples of futile praying would be the praying for a war to stop without further action by the person praying. Man himself can stop the war. He started it. He pursued it. He can stop it. The means are available to him if he will but use it. We pray for good government, for our leaders, etc., etc., but here again these are men with all of the God-given talents, and if they use them in error, and we as citizens permit it, then it is within our control and all we need do is once more use our God-given talents. We pray against the inevitable, death when it is a time to die, victory in war when there should be no war, health when we have abused our bodies and diseased our seed, happiness when we commit acts and say things that hurt others, thereby bringing unhappiness to them and to ourselves. On and on we pray for things that result from our own attitudes, or own acts, and our own disobedience. These are futile prayers and ought not to be prayed at all. Instead, we should be praying prayers of thanksgiving, of faith, hope, and charity, for strength, for wisdom and most of all for a contrite heart.

Norman Vincent Peale wrote: "If you are not getting answers to your prayers, check yourself very thoroughly and honestly as to whether you have resentments in your mind. Spiritual power cannot pass through a personality where resentment exists. Hate is a non-conductor of spiritual energy. I suggest that every time you pray you add this phrase: 'Lord, take from my thought all ill will, grudges, hates, jealousies.' Then practice casting these things from your thoughts."

Prayer is the means by which the soul communicates directly with God. It provides a basis for fellowship and an awareness of His presence. Your soul can soar upon unbelievable wings to heights never before known when one realizes that he is actually in communication with God. It provides a basis and a way of telling God how happy we are, how good we feel, and how thankful we are. Prayer is not for the sole purpose of carrying problems and complaints to God, but rather it is a path of communication and understanding. One might well call it meditation if they prefer, but to me communication with God constitutes prayer.

Isaiah states: "They that wait upon the Lord shall renew their strength; they shall mount up with wings as eagles; they shall run, and not be weary; and they shall walk and not faint." Prayer is also remaining silent, thereby permitting God to talk to us. It is not the mere mouthing off of ideas and feelings or desires and wishes, but rather a personal, confidential thing. This is why we are told to go into a closet and close the door when we pray. This is why lovers whisper into each other's ears. It is personal and between them and only them. This may be why the poet said, "Be still, my heart."

Prayer is not a time for the setting down of terms and conditions, such as "Dear God, if you will but grant me this prayer, I will go to church," or "If you will give me what I ask, I will abide by your wishes and be faithful." *Prayer is not a bargaining table. It is not a negotiating session.* Prayer should be, "Thy will be done, I ask these things, but if You do not grant them, if You do not respond, then I am well pleased and I thank You for Your wisdom. Though I may be disappointed and may not understand, nevertheless I willingly accept without complaint Your decision, and if I should cry, dear God, do not misunderstand, for how often have I denied my own children and had them cry, only to come unto me for comfort in my arms and I denied them not. I know that if I come to You for comfort, even if in Thy wisdom you denied my prayer, I know that You too will comfort me."

We should listen very carefully to class prayers and prayers given by the minister from the pulpit. We do not always agree with their prayers. *Prayer is a purely personal matter between God and man.* A Christian's group prayer should never be one of a "cheerleader" getting the most from the fans.

Prayers for needs, wants and desires would cease if man would but love God with all his heart, with all his soul, and with all his mind, and love his neighbor as himself, which are the two great commandments of the Bible. If he would substitute self-restraint for self-assertion, cease thrusting aside or treading down all competitors and give all men respect and help, if he would cease following the doctrine of survival of the fittest and seek ways for all to survive, if he would repudiate the doctrine of force for settling world problems, if he would strive to see that each man shall enjoy the benefits and advantages of our society and be mindful of those who make them possible, the great and the small, the high and the lowly, if he would look to the protection and welfare of all men and not just his own, if he would just use the intelligence and influences that his Creator gave to him in the ways intended, then he could do something about curbing the instincts and savagery of civilized man, which causes so many to pray. If he would but cease loving wordly things he would know true love. When a thing is not loved it cannot become the heart's desire, no quarrels will arise concerning it, no sadness will be felt if he loses it, no envy if it is possessed by another and not himself, no fear, no hatred—in short, no disturbances of the mind that cause men to pray.

If men would but abide by the laws of God, then they would pray prayers of love, of thanksgiving, and of praise for life, and vanished would be the prayers of wants, of hurts, and of desires. To love God is man's highest happiness and blessedness, the ultimate end and aim of all his actions. If he loves god, he will turn aside from the loves of the flesh, to the loves of the spirit, and will then, and only then, know and experience the divine love of God through prayer.

XVI

God's Promises

Some of God's promises are not fully understood. For example, many people believe that when God promised Abraham that it would be through his seed that the Saviour would be born, that this promise carried with it special considerations and benefits reserved exclusively for the Jew. They believe that this made the Jews something special and that as a result they are God's chosen people, *for wordly benefits as well as spiritual*. This assumption is partially correct, because the Jewish race was chosen for three basic reasons: (1) to bear the seed of Christ; (2) to spread the word of God to all the tribes of Israel and to the Jews; and (3) to give the word of God to the Gentiles, through the Jewish people. The assumption is partially incorrect, because the selection of the Jewish race to perform the above function has been expanded by many to mean that it carried with it special benefits and blessings, to the extent that they would be protected from the world.

Any student of Jewish history will tell you that the Jewish race has not been protected from the hardships of this world; indeed, it would appear that they have suffered more than any other single race in history. Their land has been overrun many times, their nation has been destroyed over and over, and they themselves carried off into captivity. The recent events in Germany during World War II do not reflect blessings to the Jewish race when related to their living in the world. Powerful forces are at this time being brought together to once more attack her, and to utterly destroy her as a nation, and they will very likely do so if God does not intervene for the purposes of carrying out His will, and not necessarily just to preseve the Jewish nation, because He has permitted to it happen many times before in history.

To this day the Jewish race stands upon the promises of God, even though they do not accept Christ as the Saviour. They believe that the Saviour contained in the promise has not yet come and that He is still to come. Their position is that Christ was not born of the seed of Abraham and, therefore, He could not have fulfilled the Abrahamic promise. The position of the Gentile and those Jews who have accepted and do accept Him as the Saviour is that He was of the seed of Abraham and therefore did fulfill the promise.

Nevertheless, *absent* the conflict as to whether Christ is the Saviour or is not the Saviour, one cannot but help admire the Jewish people for their absolute belief in God and in His promise. They have taken the worst that life and events can hand out to them. Throughout their history they have lost loved ones, families, their nation, their lives, but they have never lost faith in God or in His promise. It is almost unbelievable that any people could suffer as much as have the Jewish people and still retain their absolute faith in God and in His promises. It is a testimony to the world that faith, once obtained, cannot be destroyed in those who truly possess it and believe.

If the Jewish position that Jesus is not the Saviour were true, *then it would mean that the Gentile has not yet been given salvation*, for it is through Him that we receive it, and it is a little beyond my comprehension that the Jewish race can believe that we, the Gentiles, who struggle so gallantly at their side in this life to combat the forces of evil, have not been given the gift of life and of salvation through Christ. But, of course, their defense is that we do not need Christ; that we, like they, stand under the law and that obedience to the laws of God is all that is required in order to obtain the gift of eternal life. This position is, to me, insufferable for two reasons: (1) if we are all under the law, then we are all guilty under the law because no man can live a perfect life and we, therefore, both Jew and Gentile, would stand condemned under the law because we are not judged by what part of the law we have kept, but by what part of the law we have broken. If we break any part of it, then we are judged under the whole law; and (2) *it is absolutely impossible for me to conceive that a mere mortal could, in his own mind, reason out the doctrine of salvation as presented to us by Christ.* It is far too wondrous a thing to have been conceived by a man and, if this is true, then it follows that it must have been divinely inspired and not otherwise.

Of course, the position can be taken that we worship a forgiving God and that if God forgives, then why the necessity of a Christ? Well, first, if there is no necessity for a Christ, then why do the Jews cling to a hope of a future Christ? And second, if God is all-forgiving, then why a hell? *There can be no favoritism under divine law, or else law itself becomes a fraud.* Under Christ we do not stand under the law; however, if we all stand under the law, then we are all doomed, for no man is capable of perfection under the law, but the wondrous promise of Christ is that even though you break the law, He will gain you acquittal before the Father if you will but love Him and accept his payment for your sins as being genuine and not counterfeit. God, in His mercy for struggling humanity, when He witnessed their pitiful struggles to obey the law, and their failure to do so, provided, through Christ, forgiveness and salvation by the mere acceptance of Him. This was an act of mercy and reflects God's love for His people. There are many who break the law, then justify it and think that what they did was not in violation of law. They never ask God for forgiveness because they delude themselves into thinking that they live good, moral and ethical lives. In reality, they breach the law every day of their lives. It is the knowledge that I do not perform law in perfection that causes me to stand upon the promises of God, as given through Christ, that "Whosoever liveth and believeth in me, through he die, yet he shall live."

Paul wrote in Romans: "The promise to Abraham and his descendants that they should inherit the world did not come through the law, but through the righteousness of faith. If it is the adherents of the law who are to be heirs, faith is null and the promise is void. For the law brings wrath, but where there is no law there is no transgression. That is why it depends on faith, in order that the promise may rest on grace and be guaranteed to all his descendants, not only to the adherents of the law . . . "

Paul also says in Romans, "For sin will have no dominion over you, since you are not under law but under grace. What then? Are we to sin because we are not under law but under grace? By no means! Do you not know that if you yield yourselves to anyone as obedient slaves, you are slaves to the one whom you obey, either of sin, which leads to death, or of obedience, which leads to righteousness?"

What Paul is saying is that *we are not* to be so smug as to take the position that we believe in Christ, therefore we are released from the law. What he means is that if we are believers in Christ we are no longer slaves to sin, but are slaves to Christ and therefore cannot do otherwise than obey Him and strive to keep the law.

Romans outlines the wondrous promises of God to those who accept and believe in Christ: "There is therefore now no condemnation for those who are in Christ Jesus. For the law of the spirit of life in Christ Jesus has set me free from the law of sin and death. For God has done what the law, weakened by the flesh, could not do; sending His own Son in the likeness of sinful flesh and for sin, He condemned sin in the flesh in order that the just requirements of the law might be fulfilled in us who walk not according to the flesh, but according to the spirit . . . To set the mind on the flesh is death, but to set the mind on the spirit is life and peace. For the mind that is set on the flesh is hostile to God; it does not submit to God's law, indeed it cannot, and those who are in the flesh cannot please God.

"But you are not in the Flesh, you are in the spirit, if the spirit of God really dwells in you. Anyone who does not have the spirit of Christ does not belong to Him. But if Christ is in you, although your bodies are dead because of sin, your spirits are alive because of righteousness. If the spirit of Him dwells in you, He who raised Christ Jesus from the dead will give life to your mortal bodies, also through His spirit which dwells in you."

We always seem to come back to the word "faith." How can we be positive that the promises of God will come about or that they are true? To say that, "I believe in the promises of God" results in a significant statement, but it does not necessarily express a statement of fact. In other words, a belief is not necessarily a fact, because it is possible to hold to a system of beliefs which, when weighed one against the other, are absolutely consistent, and yet the fact that the beliefs are consistent does not prove that all of them are not false, or that all of them are true. Just because one declares that his belief is "true" does not make it so, but means that it is "true" only insofar as it is entertained by him, and the belief fits in with the sum total of his beliefs and knowledge.

We all adapt our minds to follow our beliefs and will order the workings of our lives to conform to those beliefs. Thus, we do not like to take into consideration any set of statements which causes us to doubt our beliefs, but prefer to entertain only those things which serve to bolster and to perpetuate our beliefs. The stronger we cling to our beliefs, the stronger they become. The more deeply embedded they are, the more difficult it is to pry them out of one's thoughts. Thus, in the broadest sense, faith means steadfastness of belief. Each of us has an absolute right to arrive at and cling to any belief that we wish, for it is an expression of free will, or the will to believe, and if another takes a contrary position, it is his right to do so. If one should inquire of us of our beliefs, we should express them. However, if they then wish to tear down or destroy our beliefs, then we are perfectly justified in telling them to hush their mouths, because the basis of our beliefs has as much validity as do theirs. To have absolute faith in the promises of God, in human immortality, and in Christ needs no justification nor defense, and can lead to satisfying the deepest cravings, hopes and aspirations of men. Our position is that we have a perfect right to hold to our convictions, and that no possibility exists which could cause us to regret a belief in the promises of God, in the saving grace of Christ, or in immortality, because if we are wrong we shall never know the least disappointment. Only what we do, the acts we commit, or the denials thereof, could quite possibly cause us to regret the contrary beliefs to which we might have come.

Are these convictions the result of fear? Well, not in the sense that we understand the word "fear," because we know that if we die and there is nothing, then we shall never be disappointed, nor be aware of the rightness or wrongness of our beliefs and hopes. On the other hand, if there is something beyond, then we might well regret our beliefs and actions. But let us assume that it is fear. *Only the greatest of idiots can claim that he has no fear of death or of the unknown.* When anyone states that he is looking forward to death, that he can hardly wait, and that it will be a great day, then our reaction is that he is a malcontent with life as we know it; that he is suffering great physical or mental pain; that he is tired of living in God's world; or that it is nothing more than a statement of bravado. A suicide does not say, "I am the happiest man in he world, without a care in the world; nevertheless I want to see God today, so I have taken my own life." If we are honest, we will admit that we fear the act of dying. When we were in school we feared being sent to the principal's office because we didn't know what to expect. It was the unknown element that we feared. There are so many things we do not know about the world beyond, that through instinct we know a tinge of fear. But that fear is swiftly moved back into the recesses of our minds because a feeling of confidence overwhelms us whenever we review the promises of God. But we are honest enough to say that if we thought we were going to die today, we'd rush to the nearest doctor or hospital for treatment and would probably pray that we not die, and even here we'd probably be justifying our pleadings on the basis that our wife needed us, or our kids needed us, or that we had a work that was unfinished, or that we could do much good for the world if we lived. But, we'd be scared, not in the sense of terror or horror, *but in the simple human instict of being fearful of the unknown.*

There is no shame in a sense of fear of death for the Christian concerning the act of dying—it is only when we do not believe in the promises of God. If we do not believe that there will be life, if we believe that we do die, that we shall not be saved, that He does not love us, that Christ is not the Saviour, then true fear exists, even to the point of being terrified! It is only when we fear that these things are true that the fear of death is wrong. But to fear death simply because we fear the act of dying is natural, normal, and even desirable from the standpoint of self-preservation. When we truly believe in the promises of God we do not fear death, per se, but only what the act of dying will be like and this is quite natural. Possibly even Christ feared the actual act of dying when He cried out on the cross, "My God, my God, why hast thou forsaken me?" Perhaps for one fleeting moment He felt fear, and this is normal for the flesh, because Christ came into the flesh as a man and He experienced all of the frailties of the flesh, and it would be quite natural for fear to be an experience which He, too, had to suffer as part payment for the souls of men.

Let's look at some of the promises of God as related to us in the Scriptures and testified to by the authors thereof. In Acts we read, "God had raised up David to be their King, of whom He testified and said, 'I have found in David, the son of Jesse, a man after my heart, who will do all my will.' Of this man's posterity God brought to Israel a Saviour, Jesus, as He promised." This is a testimony that God made a promise and that He kept it.

Acts also recorded, "And we bring to you the goodness that what God promised to the fathers, this He has fulfilled to us their children by raising Jesus." Again, a promise and a fulfillment.

Hebrews: "For when God made a promise to Abraham, since He had no one greater by whom to swear, He swore to Himself, saying, 'Surely I will bless you and multiply you.' And thus Abraham, having patiently endured, obtained the promise." A promise made, a promise kept.

Then we have the promises of eternal life. In Titus we read, "Paul, a servant of God and an apostle of Jesus Christ, to further the faith of God's elect and their knowledge of truth which accords with godliness in hope of eternal life which God, who never lies, promised ages ago."

Timothy: "Paul, an apostle of Christ Jesus by the will of God according to the promise of the life which is in Christ Jesus."

Hebrews: "And how much shall the blood of Christ, who through the eternal Spirit offered Himself without blemish to God, purify your conscience from dead works to serve the living God. Therefore He is the mediator of a new covenant, so that those who are called may receive the promised eternal inheritance, since a death has occurred which redeems them from the transgressions under the first covenent."

1 John: "And this is what He has promised us, eternal life."

Well, to whom was the promise of eternal life made?

Acts: "Repent, and be baptized every one of you in the name of Jesus Christ for the forgiveness of your sins; *and you shall receive the gift of the Holy Spirit. For the promise is to you and to your children and to all that are far off, every one whom the Lord our God calls to him.*"

Ephesians: "That is how the Gentiles are fellow heirs, members of the same body, and partakers of the promise in Christ Jesus through the gospel."

Galatians: "There is neither Jew nor Greek, there is neither slave nor free, there is neither male nor female, for you are all one in Christ Jesus. And if you are Christ's then you are Abraham's offspring, heirs according to promise."

You know, sometimes we grow impatient, we feel that things move too slowly, we sometimes feel that evil ought to be brought to a swift and sudden end and we grow weary of waiting for the promises to be fulfilled and our restless hearts quieted forever. But Peter explains this feeling of impatience: "But do not ignore this one fact, beloved, that with the Lord one day is as a thousand years, and a thousand years as one day. The Lord is not slow about his promises as some count slowness, but is forbearing toward you, not wishing that any should perish but that all should reach repentance."

I do not know how you feel, but I am certainly glad that He waits for me because I have a long way to go and my end might come too soon and I might die in defeat rather than in victory!

We must develop patience and confidence and take he same position set out in Peter: "But according to His promise we wait for new happiness and a new earth in which righteousness dwells."

There is a great sympathy for us in the Bible and we are given words of assurance and encouragement.

Hebrews states: "Therefore do not throw away your confidence, which has a great reward. For you have need of endurance so that you may do the will of God *and receive what is promised.*"

XVII

Christian Responsibilities

"I am a Christian." This is probably one of the easiest things that one can say if he has been reared in a Christian nation, of Christian parentage, and if, from childhood, he has attended a Christian church. It is as easy to say as "I am an American," because we were born in America; thus we are Americans. But the problem is, how strong a Christian are we? Can we stand up to our adversaries? In times of stress do we abandon our Christian heritage and retreat into our inner selves, taking the position that we have done all that we can do to save our fellow man, but he will not hear, so we will not battle on behalf of Christ or God, but will take the easy way out and simply withdraw from our responsibility?

Elijah was faced with this very situation and in Kings we read the following:

"And there he came to a cave, and lodged there; and behold, the word of the Lord came to him and He said to him, 'What are you doing here, Elijah?' He said, 'I have been very jealous for the Lord, the God of Hosts; for the people of Israel have forsaken thy covenant, thrown down thy altars, and slain thy prophets with the sword; and I, even I only, am left; and they seek my life, to take it away.' And God said, 'Go forth and stand upon the mount before the Lord.' And behold, the Lord passed by and a great and strong wind rent the mountains, and broke in pieces the rocks before the Lord, but the Lord was not in the wind; and after the wind an earthquake, but the Lord was not in the earthquake; and after the fire a still, small voice. And when Elijah heard it he wrapped his face in his mantle and went out and stood at the entrance of the cave. And behold, there came a voice to him and said, 'What are you doing here, Elijah?' He said, 'I have been very jealous for the Lord, the God of Hosts, for the people of Israel have forsaken thy covenants, thrown down thy altars, and slain thy prophets with the sword; and I, even I only, am left, and they seek my life to take it away.' And the Lord said to him, 'Go, return on your way to the wilderness of Damascus; and when you arrive you shall anoint Hazael to be king over Syria, and Jehu the son of Nimshi you shall anoint to be king over Israel, and Elisha the son of Shaphat of Abelmeholah you shall anoint to be prophet in your place. And him who escapes from the sword of Hazael shall Jehu slay, and him who escapes from the sword of Jehu shall Elisha slay. Yet I will leave seven thousand in Israel, all the knees that have not bowed to Baal, and every mouth that has not kissed him."

Thus we find Elijah fleeing from the strife of life and retreating from his responsibilities, but God sends him back into the battle with orders to fulfill his charge. He did not go back as the result of flaming manifestoes, or because of ravings of radicals, or the shoutings of politicians, or the criers of doom. He heard a great wind, and then an earthquake, and finally a great fire, but the Lord was not in the wind, not in the earthquake, and not in the fire, but in a still, small voice. God made His power known to Elijah, and His will in a still, small voice, and it was to this voice that Elijah listened. God told him to return to the struggle to establish truth and purity and holiness in the life of the people of God, and Elijah obeyed. Too often we listen to he wild ravings of men who shout so loud that we cannot hear the still, small voice speaking to us. We listen to our own loud rantings, of our own desire to establish ourselves as persons of great Scriptural knowledge and in our ego we do not hear that still, small voice speaking to us, pleading, telling us not to abandon our principles of faith in the face of modern onslaughts. It would have been easy for Elijah to have answered, "No, I will not return to the struggle, I have done enough, I have done all I can and they will not listen. If this is the way things are going to turn out after all I have done, then I quit. "But he did not; he stopped and in quiet stillness listened to the still, small voice.

We could also adopt the same position and simply leave the struggle and join the forces that oppose us either by words or by deeds, or we can continue in the struggle to inform our fellows of the will of God and tell them of His love. Not by rantings, ravings, speeches, cries of doom and all the rest that we have become so familiar with, but in quiet voices and with firm resolve we can stand fast in the face of all that oppose us and do, to the extent that we can, what we know to be the will of God.

And we have our guidelines as to the will of God in the Ten Commandments, the Sermon on the Mount, and in the Golden Rule. And we could add I Corinthians 13: "If I speak of God and of angels but have not love, I am a noisy gong or a clanging cymbal. And if I have prophetic powers, and understand all knowledge and all mysteries, and if I have faith, so as to remove mountains, but have not love, I am nothing. If I give away all I have, and if I deliver my body to be burned, but have not love, I gain nothing."

And from Galatians: "But the fruit of the spirit is love, joy, peace, patience, kindness, goodness, faithfulness, gentleness, self-control, against such there is no law and those who belong to Christ Jesus have crucified the flesh with its passions and desires. If we live by the spirit, let us also walk by the spirit. Let us have no self-conceit, no provoking of one another, no envy of one another." And from Philippians: "Have this mind among yourselves, which you have in Christ Jesus, who, though He was in the form of God, He did not count equality with God a thing to be grasped, but emptied himself, taking the form of a servant being born in the likeness of men. And being found in human form He humbled Himself and became obedient unto death, even death on the cross." These are but some of the things that conform to the will of God; they are not absolutes, but they do form the guidelines for our lives and they must be taken into consideration before coming to decisions regarding our conduct and whether what we do conforms to the will of God.

We have other guidelines, as found in Romans: "let us conduct ourselves becomingly as in the day, not in reveling and drunkenness, not in debauchery and licentiousness, not in quarreling and jealousy, but put on the Lord Jesus Christ and make no provision for the flesh to gratify its desire." And in Corinthians: "Shun immorality. Every other sin which a man commits is outside the body, but the immoral man sins against his own body. Do you not know that your body is a temple of the Holy Spirit within you, which you have from God? You are not your own, you were bought with a price, so glorify God in your body. Now the works of the flesh are plain: immorality, impurity, licentiousness, idolatry, sorcery, enmity, strife, jealousy, anger, selfishness, dissension, party spirit, envy, drunkenness, carousing, and the like." And also Ephesians: "Therefore, do not be foolish, but understand what is the will of God, and do not get drunk with wine, for that is debauchery, but be filled with the spirit addressing one another in psalms and hymns and spiritual songs, singing and making melody to the Lord with all your heart, always and for everything giving thanks in the name of our Lord Jesus Christ to God the Father."

Whenever I hear someone say, "I do not know what is the will of God or what it is He wants of me, or how I am to know that what I do is in conformity with the will of God," then I know it is indicative of *one who has not read the Scriptures* and that if he truly wanted to know the will of God, I mean truly wanted to know, he would do so. True, these guidelines do not provide specific answers to every situation with which we are faced in life; nevertheless, they do provide guidelines which do enable the Christian to make a responsible decision in any situation.

If we will but stop for a moment when we are faced with a decision to listen to the small voice that speaks within us, we will become aware of the presence of the Holy Spirit in our lives, for it gently, quietly prods and guides us in all that we do and we can feel it rejoice when we do right and grieve when we do wrong. A man of God knows what is right and what is wrong, and if anyone professes that he does not know the will of God and wishes to know the will of God, *then he will dedicate some time each day to the Scriptures*. He will ferret out those passages that pertain to His will and to what He expects of us and what we should expect of ourselves before we can truly say, "I am a Christian."

There are many whose quality of life and whose commitment to Christ belies their profession of faith, and there are others to whom we can go with our problems and heartaches and find compassion, understanding, and knowledge in the ways of God, and who will deny themselves for our sake. They are there, usually in the background, quiet people, yet somehow we know that we could turn to them in times of despair and trouble and that they will respond. It is in them that there is hope for mankind; no matter how far afield men go in their affairs, there is always a remant of men and women who stand fast and will not yield to the pressures of living in conformity or to those who would destroy all that we hold to be true.

You do not find them on soap boxes, they are not great orators, they do not lead demonstrations, or participate in rioting and rebellion, but when the dust has settled they come forth and quietly put man back on the right track and gently, quietly prod them towards a return to the sane and a return to God. You do not know them, but they are there. You will recall that in the passage I read about Elijah it closes with the words, "Yet I will leave seven thousand in Israel all the knees not bowed to Baal, and every mouth that has not kissed him." These were the remnants, we do not know their names or their deeds, they did not become famous, but these were quiet men and women who stood fast. They are always there, for they are those who are truly men and women of God and they will always rise up and return men to sanity and place mankind back on the road that leads to goodness and godliness. Some of these men and women you know; most you do not, but they are there, they have always been there, and they will always be there in the future. You cannot issue a call that they come to you for they will not respond, but they will find you, of this you may be assured and there exists between them strange recognition even though no word is spoken. I have met them and I know them, and so do you. They do not throw Scripture about in proof of what they believe. They are not noisy people but they are quiet people, yet their very presence can be sensed. You know by what they do not say that they are honest, sincere, and truly men and women of God. There are many, and they know one another even though no word has passed between them, they met, shook hands, and knew.

In the Book of Psalms we read of these men and women: "Blessed is the man what walketh not in the counsel of the ungodly, nor standeth in the way of sinners, nor sitteth in the seat of the scornful, but his delight is in the law of the Lord and in His law doth he meditate day and night. And he shall be like a tree planted by the rivers of water, that bringeth forth his fruit in his season, his leaf also shall not wither, and whatsoever he doeth shall prosper. The ungodly are not so, but are like the chaff which the wind driveth away. Therefore the ungodly shall not stand in the judgment, nor sinners in the congregation of the righteous. For the Lord knoweth the way of the righteous, but the way of the ungodly shall perish."

These men and women know each other and they are also known to God, and they know God. They do not fade away but stand fast. Christ said, "I am the Good Shepherd, and I know my sheep, and am known of mine. As the Father knoweth me, even so I the Father, and I lay down my life for the sheep. And other sheep I have, which are not of this fold, them also I must bring and they shall hear my voice, and there shall be one fold and one shepherd."

Steadfastness is one of the most important qualities that a Christian can develop. The Christians who died in the arena of Rome on the cross, eaten by wild animals, burned at the stake, and hacked to pieces by Roman torturers, stood fast. Those who withstood the terrible tortures of the Spanish Inquisition stood fast. It is not always easy to do so, even on a small scale. We are inclined to water down our beliefs so as to be acceptable in our society. We fear the brand of snob, of the name do-gooder. We compromise our beliefs in order to gain acceptance and we are always careful not to be branded a religious fanatic or some kind of nut. We proclaim loudly the graduation of a son or daughter from college, but not our conversion. We extol the virtues of books like *The Naked ape* and *The Godfather*, but not the Holy Bible. We buy all the latest publications and then sit down and read them from cover to cover, but we buy the Holy Bible and place it on a shelf, never to be read. We thump our chests and proclaim that we are a Democrat or a Republican, but not the fact that we are Christians. We invite our friends out for the evening for drinking and eating, but we do not invite them to church. We restrict our conversation about God and Christ and church to those who are already members of the church and who we know are already believers, but we do not engage the stranger or business assoicate or passing acquaintance in religious discussion. It is taboo to do so, and we fear that there will be whispering behind our backs about our sanity. But all do not do so, and these are the remnants upon which the world depends for survival.

We put our trust in God; shouldn't He be able to put His trust in us? *He is not ashamed to be called our God, so should we be ashamed to call Him our God?* He was not afraid to sacrifice the life of His Son so that we might have life; should we not likewise be unafraid to sacrifice our time, our lives, so that that life was not given in vain? World pressures are growing every day and it will become more and more difficult to stand fast. We must resolve now that we will take the same vow that Paul took when he wrote:

"I consider that the sufferings of this present time are not worth comparing with the glory that is to be revealed to us."

And also:

"For I am persuaded that neither death, nor life, nor angels, nor principalities, nor powers, nor things present, nor things to come, nor height, nor depth, nor any other creature shall be able to separate us from the love of God, which is in Christ Jesus our Lord."

Our strength will come to test, our love will be challenged, our hearts' desires will be shattered, we will learn how to weep, and we will know heartache. But if we stand fast we will inherit that which no man can give, nor take away, eternal life with our Lord Jesus Christ.

Do not think that the Christian has been promised protection from the hardships of the world. We were born to live in the world, to struggle in it, and then to die and pass from it. There are no hardships suffered by others that we, too, will not suffer; there are no tears wept by others that we shall not also weep; we are not immune from the sufferings of this world, but we are of the world and it is here that we shall live and die. Indeed, the Christian suffers more than others, for we cannot look upon suffering humanity and not suffer a little ourselves. Their struggles become our struggles and their heartaches, ours. This is one of the penalties we pay as the result of being Christians, for we would, if we could, lift up the hearts of men so that all would know of the promise of eternal life offered by Christ to all that will but take it. He is the ultimate hope of the world and it is in this knowledge that we find peace and joy in the midst of turmoil. It is this message that makes our hearts yearn that all men should know, and we suffer for them. We would have all men know the words recorded in Revelation:

Behold, the dwelling place of God is with men, He will dwell with them, and they shall be His people, and God Himself will be with them. He will wipe away every tear from their eyes, and death shall be no more; neither shall there be mourning nor crying nor pain anymore, for the former things have passed away. Behold, I make all things new. Write this for these words are trustworthy and true, it is done! I am the alpha and the omega, the beginning and the end. To the thirsty I will give water without price from the fountain of the water of life. He who conquers shall have this heritage, and I will be his God and he shall be My son."

And we will be the sons and daughters of God if we will but stand steadfast in our love for God and for each other. This is the greatest of all dreams that men can dream, and it should be the total sum and substance of our heart's desire.

Christ said: "I am the true vine, and my Father is the vinedresser. Every branch of mine that bears no fruit, He takes away, and every branch that does bear fruit He prunes, that it may bear more fruit. You are already made clean by the word which I have spoken to you. Abide in me, and I in you. As the branch cannot bear fruit by itself, unless it abides in the vine, neither can you, unless you abide in me. *I am the vine, you are the branches.* He who abides in me, and I in him, he is it that bears much fruit. If a man does not abide in me, he is cast forth as a branch and withers, and the branches are gathered, thrown in the fire and burned. If you abide in me, and my words abide in you, ask whatever you will, and it shall be done for you. By this my Father is glorified, that you bear much fruit, and so prove to be my disciples."

The word "abide" means to endure, to remain, stay, dwell, or reside, continue, stand firm, to adhere or conform to, to wait for. When Christ abides in one then he must face squarely his involvement in this life with other men, he cannot be "an island unto himself." Either he will bear fruit, or wither and die. *Everything a man does in this life acts either for the good or ill of other men*, and this, in turn, has an effct upon one's own sense of well-being. When we conform to the love of Christ, then we act as a powerful influence upon all those who come into contact with us. This influence extends to our political, social, racial, national, and religious lives, and it is through these activities that we come into contact with our fellow human beings. It is in these areas that we exert our greatest influence upon others, and it is here that we must reflect our abiding love for Christ, so that all can see and know the tremendous impact that Christ has upon a person's life. This, in turn, if we properly reflect the love of Christ, will cause men to pause and to take note and strive to pattern their lives more in tune with ours, and this can lead them to Christ. This is our charge, our mandate, and we must not abort our mission.

One of the most important traits that we must reflect is that what we do is not for reward, but rather our concern with good works is an expression of the fact that in Christ we are saved. *Good works are the fruit of the vine, not the roots.*

The words of Christ which are from John illustrate the close relationship that the disciples had with Christ, and it is this relationship that we must always strive to establish. Two figures of speech were used in the above passages: one is a word picture of the vine and the branches, representing, of course, Christ as the vine, and we as the branches. The second is the word "abide."

The use of the word "vine," as meaning the heart of a thing, is not new in the Bible. For example, Israel is often compared to a vine because it is through her that Christianity is founded, and it is through her that the word of Christ was given to the Gentiles. "Thou hast brought a vine out of Egypt, thou hast cast out the heathen, and planted it. Thou preparest room before it, and didst cause it to take deep root, and it filled the land. The hills were covered with the shadow of it, and the boughs thereof were like the goodly cedars. She sent out her boughs unto the sea, and her branches unto the river."

Isaiah speaks of the vineyard when he writes of God's judgment upon sins. "Now will I sing to my well-beloved a song, a song to my beloved touching his vineyard. My well-beloved hath a vineyard in a very fruitful hill. And he fenced it, and gathered out the stones thereof, and planted it with the choicest vine, and built a tower in the midst of it, and also made a winepress therein, and he looked that it should bring forth grapes, and it brough forth wild grapes. And now, O inhabitants of Jerusalem, and men of Judah, judge, I pray you, between me and my vineyard. What could have been done more to my vineyard that I have not done in it? Wherefore, when I looked that it should bring forth grapes, brought it forth wild grapes? And now go, I will tell you what I will do to my vineyard, I will take away the hedge thereof, and it shall be eaten up; and break down the wall thereof, and it shall be trodden down, and I will lay it waste, it shall not be pruned, nor digged, but there shall come up briers and thorns, I will also command the clouds that they rain no rain upon it. For the vineyard of the Lord is the house of Israel and the men of Judah his pleasant plant, and he looked for judgement, but beheld oppression, for righteousness, but beheld a cry.''

A true vine is perfectly in harmony with its intended nature. Jesus is the true vine because of His perfect relationship with God, and it is this relationship that we must always strive to attain, to the extent that mortals can do so. There is a story of the vine which illustrates our relationship with man.

''In the spring the vine pushes up from the soil and sends forth its tentacle towards the sky, seeking something upon which to climb. If it can find none, it begins to crawl among the weeds and continue on its way. If, at last, it finds a pole upon which it can climb, it will do so, reaching upward and outward towards the sun. If the pole should be a rotten one, it will collapse beneath the weight of the vine and the vine will once more find itself among the weeds. If, however, the pole is a strong one, the vine will grow into its full majesty under the sun and bring forth much fruit.''

We must all, at all times, be certain that we are a strong pole, and that we are strong enough for the vine of humanity to climb upon, and grow into its full nobility; if we collapse, then the vine will collapse, and we all, both ourselves and the vine, will sink back into the mire and rot away.

When individuals abide in Christ and He in them, then they reflect His presence in all that they do. You can feel the strength in them, and somehow you know that Christ permeates their thoughts in all that they say and do. They are the ones who witness to Christ, to the Scriptures, to the wonders of worship, and to the fellowship of believers. These are the salt of the earth, the sturdy vine. They are not necessrily those who merely profess belief in God, and go through the motions of religion, because Christ said, ''Not everyone who says to me, 'Lord, Lord' shall enter the kingdon of Heaven, but he who does the will of my Father who is in Heaven.''

You can tell those in whom Christ abides, for they are imitators of Him, bearing much fruit, forgiving their enemies, loving their fellow men, worshiping God through word, act, and deed, and they are obedient to Him. Obedience may be the wrong term to apply to the Christian, for it seems to apply to law, or following orders, compulsion and not a wholehearted response, out of love. *Probably a better word would be co-workers.*

People who work with Christ find joy and happiness in serving Him and in doing His work. It is most important that one does work with Christ, because our shadow and influence falls across the lives of all those with whom we come in contact. We have a high calling, that we make our influence count for truth and righteousness in the lives of all those we meet. We come into contact with those who are morally confused, grieved over personal losses, who worry about their defects, and over their defeats. We meet lonely people and those who long for friendship and understanding. Some are in desperate need of a few of the necessities of life, or a kind word, or just our presence. Some seek after God and an understanding of Christ. All about us, humanity groans and it is we, the branches of the vine, to whom they can look and in whom they place their hope. *When we serve mankind, we serve God.* Christ said, "For which is the greater, one who sits at the table, or the one who serves? Is it not the one who sits at the table? But I am among you as one who serves."

When we serve mankind with all our strength and all our efforts, and when we do all that Christ would ask of us, then we are not servants of Him, but of man, and in this there is a wondrous thing. Christ told the disciples of those who serve, "This is my commandment, that ye love one another as I have loved you. Greater love has no man than this, that a man lay down his life for his friends. Ye are my friends, if ye do whatsoever I command you. Henceforth I call you not servants, for the servant knoweth not what his lord doeth, but I have called you friends for all things that I have heard of my father I have made known unto you. You have not chosen me, but I have chosen you, and ordained you, that you should go and bring forth fruit, and that your fruit should remain, that whatsoever ye shall ask of the Father in my name, He may give it to you. These things I command you, that you love one another."

A friend is one who is attached to another by feelings of personal regard, a supporter, one who is on good terms with another. To be a friend one must have characteristics of, or befitting, a friend. When one says, "I am your friend," it means that he approves of you. We are not at all sure we are Christ's friend, for if we do not approve of all that we do, how could He? Nevertheless, to be his friend should be one of the primary goals of our lives. How does one become Christ's friend? He said, *"Ye are my friends, if ye do whatever I command you."* My weakness is that I do not always do what He commands me to do.

Many people develop the feeling that it is too late for them, that they have lived evil lives, that they are late in years, and that they should have accepted Christ and abided by His words in their youth. Although they feel that they have been forgiven, they feel that those who labored long for the Lord will receive greater reward, and they are remorseful about their misspent youth. But not so! Christ told a parable that should dispel any such notion from anyone who labors under such false conclusions.

"For the kingdom of Heaven is like unto a man that is a householder, which went out early in the morning to hire laborers into his vineyard. And when he had agreed with the laborers for a penny a day, he sent them into the vineyard. And he went out about the third hour, and saw others standing idle in the market place, and said unto them, go ye also into the vineyard, and whatsoever is right I will give you. And they went their way. Again, he went out about the sixth and ninth hour, and did likewise. And about the eleventh hour he went out, and found others standing idle, and said unto them, "Why stand ye here all the day idle?

"They said unto him, 'Because no man has hired us.'

"He said unto them, 'Go ye also into the vineyard, and whatsoever is right, that shall ye receive'

"So when even was come, the lord of the vineyard said until his steward, 'Call the laborers, and give them their hire, beginning from the last unto the first.'

"And when they came that were hired about the eleventh hour they received every man a penny. But when the first came, they supposed that they should have received more, and they likewise received every man a penny. And when they had received it, they murmured against the good-man of the house saying, 'These last have wrought but one hour, and thou has made them equal unot us, which have borne the burden and heat of the day.'

"But he answered one of them, and said, 'Friend, I do thee no wrong; didst not thou agree with me for a penny? Take what is thine and go thy way, I will give unto this last, even as unto thee. Is it not lawful for me to do what I will with mine own? Is thine eye evil, because I am good? So the last shall be first, and the first last, for many be called, but few chosen.' "

It is never too late to serve Christ, to accept His saving grace or to do His work. Even if that work is only for a short time, suppose in that short span you bring one man to Christ? Wouldn't it be enough? One should never look back. but forward, for as Omar Khayyam wrote:

> "The moving finger writes; and, having write,
> Moves on; nor all your piety nor wit
> Shall lure it back to cancel half a line,
> Nor all your tears wash out a word of it."

Christ put no time limit upon the forgiveness of sins; neither did He put a stumbling block in the way of any man who would do good works, and He loves the large branch of the vine as well as the new shoot. *Life is not yesterday, it is today, and, perhaps, tomorrow.* These are but some of the messages that we must tell our fellows if we would serve Christ and be a branch of the vine.

We all remember the parable of the ten pieces of silver: "Either what woman, having ten pieces of silver, if she lose one piece, doth not light a candle, and sweep the house, and seek diligently till she find it? And when she hath found it, she calleth her friends and neighbors together, saying, 'Rejoice with me, for I have found that piece which I had lost.' Likewise, I say unto you, there is joy in the presence of the angels of God over one sinner that repenteth."

No time limit, no age bracket, just a sinner who was lost and then was found. That is the fruit that we must bear if we are to be a branch of the vine.

We have all noticed that throughout the growing season a vine continues to grow, to put out its tentacles, its blossoms, and then brings forth its fruit, and it is not until the growing season is over that the vine stops its activities. And so it is with our lives. As long as we live in our allotted time, we must do that which is worthy of God, and bear good fruit until it is time for us to go.

Tennyson wrote the following:

> "Sunset and evening star,
> And one clear call for me!
> And may there be no moaning at the bar
> When I put out to sea.
> For tho' from out our borne of time and place
> The floods may bear me far,
> I hope to see my Pilot—face to face,
> When I have crossed the bar.

As any vine must be watered, and fed, in order to survive and bear fruit, so must the soul be fed and watered and the water of life for the soul is contained in these words: "Verily, verily, I say unto you, he hath heareth my word, and believeth on Him that sent me, hath everlasting life, and shall not come into condemnation, but is passed from death unto life."

XVIII

Heaven and Hell

In the modern church, the use of the word "hell" is almost a no-no. After all, we are much to sophisticated to speak of hell, and beside, it is an irritating subject. It is to be avoided because it really belongs with the ignorant and in the realm of superstition. It is perfectly all right to speak of reward and punishment, of heaven, of love, and of things pleasant to hear, but to speak of hell—that is taboo. We are inclined to adopt the position of the ostrich and say, there is no hell.

Some people will go to great lengths to avoid a discussion of hell. It makes them feel uncomfortable and, anyway, they feel that there is something unjust about a hell. It goes against their moral fiber. The difficulty is that we, in our own vanity, tend to feel that a God of Love could not be less compassionate than we are, and we are by our own admission most assuredly compassionate. We could not condemn a man to eternal hell, no matter what he had done, thus the proper conclusion is that, therefore, God could not do so. Unfortunately, such a conclusion cannot be supported and is in error, mainly because most people simply will not try to understand anything about hell and, therefore, reject the concept altogether. This is not difficult to understand because most of what we were taught when young and impressionable is not accurate, when one examines and thoughtfully applies the Scriptures to the meaning of hell.

Some, while refusing to entertain any thought about hell, do, nevertheless, tend to accept what they were taught but then push it back into the recesses of their mind and try to justify hell on the basis that hell only exists on this earth, in this life, but in the afterlife there is no hell, *only a heaven*. This is wishful thinking and such a conclusion fits very neatly in with our sense of justice. *There is, of course, nothing wrong with this conclusion, except that it cannot be supported by the Scriptures!* Such a conclusion is pure conjecture and is based upon assumptions designed to vindicate God and to soothe one's inner revolt against the existence of eternal hell, and it does not necessitate their rejecting their understanding of the reference of hell in the Bible. It is a comfortable position to take.

There are many who charge that we believe in and fear hell, and that is why we worship God in the first place—out of fear. Researchers into the origin of religion have come to the conclusion that primitive man endowed natural phenomena with life, and having done so then ascribed personalities to them. These supernatural powers were to be feared and, if one could please them, there would be no fear because the powers would then intervene on their behalf, and only good could result. Their claim is that the basis of religion is to be found in man's awe in the presence of the extraordinary and terrifying events of nature, and that fear ensued and that men do all they can to placate their God so as not to incur His wrath or judgment in accordance with their works.

We have also heard the charge made that if there is a hell, then our God must be the greatest of monsters to condemn a man to eternity in hell, full of everlasting torment, fire, and brimstone. With this charge we would agree that if our God did such a thing, it would most assuredly be ture, but such is not the case, based upon the Scriptures and not upon some whim of our own. *It is not the intent to try to alter your beliefs or to justify God, nor to vindicate Him*, but merely to bring out what the Scriptures say when superstition has been stripped away and you will once more see that, as in all research concerning the nature of God, He needs neither justification nor vindication. *What is needed is understanding on our part.*

What does the word "hell" mean? The word "hell" is generally used in the Old Testament to translate the Hebrew word 'sheol," which simply means the place of the dead, without reference to either reward or punishment. In the new Testament, the word "hell" is used to translate two words, "Hades," generally meaning the same as Sheol, the place of the dead, and "Gehenna," the place of retribution for evil deeds. The word in its basic meaning means "the abode of the dead," "the place of departed spirits," "the grave." How did this meaning develop into a concept of punishment?

Most men have a fear of death and it was quite natural for the religious teachers of long ago, and even in modern times, to use the word "hell," meaning death, so as to instill fear and to gain obedience to their doctrines. Thus, instead of saying that the sinner would simply die and go to the grave, they substituted the word "hell" for the word "grave" and then, to give it even greater impact and to instill an even greater fear, they added to its meaning.

That fear has been, and is still being used by teachers and priests in the past and present to gain obedience to their doctrines cannot be denied. It is from this position that the idea of hell and fire and brimstone ensued. Fire, out of control, is an awesome thing and its injuries are horrible and hurtful. It is capable of destroying all that comes in its way, and even under proper conditions can convert solid rock into huge, terrifying flows of red-hot lava. A forest fire is terrifying to man and to all living creatures of the forest; it is a thing that demands respect. Fire is quite capable of instilling fear in the hearts of men and it became natural, when seeking something to add to the fear of death or hell and to instill greater fear into the hearts of men in order to force obedience, to add fire. Death and fire both are feared from natural means and were quite adaptable to being incorporated into religious beliefs to that fear could be instilled and obedience obtained.

Now, to this picture add the third element—eternity. No hope, no relief, no chance for parole, *forever*. This idea was developed by those who observed that the dumps around the cities, much as they are today, when they caught fire burned on and on or, if you wish, eternally, being always fed with more refuse. In those days when animals died they were tossed into the city dump; likewise, when a person died and no one claimed his body, it, too, was thrown into the city dump to be consumed by the fire. This is where the expression, "even the worms shall follow you into hell' evolved. If the body did not come into contact with the fire, the worms invaded it. This was a terrible end, an awful fate that could befall one, to be unloved and merely tossed into the city dump. One must always remember that much of the Old Testament was the result of priests and teachers realizing that they taught a people who could neither read nor write and who could barely reason for themselves and who had to rely upon the teachers for knowledge. Being ignorant, they could understand what they saw and felt, and they could easily understand what they were being taught if they could associate it with something with which they were familiar. Thus, in many cases, teachers used a combination of ignorance and fear to put over their points. They used symbolic language, language the ignorant could understand. They feared death, they knew what fire could do, they had seen the eternal fires of the city dump, they had seen the bodies of unloved ones tossed into the city dump, they could understand that this would be a terrible end to one's life. So, the word "hell" was used in relation to death, punishment, fire, brimstone, and eternity, and the combined word usage of hellfire came into being with the passage of time. What could instill more terror into the hearts of the simple-minded masses of those days than having some religious man pointing the finger of accusation at some poor soul and roaring, "You are going to hell where you will burn forever for your acts, and there you will burn in hell forever and ever." *It must have frightened the poor devils out of their wits!*

But omitting superstition and false teachings, what does the Bible truly say of heaven and hell?

Well, first it should be remembered that Christ is referred to as the Light of the World, and Satan is referred to as the Prince of Darkness.

I would like to give you a saying of Christ and ask that you keep it in mind: "Yet a little while is the light with you, walk while ye have the light, lest darkness come upon you, for he that walketh in darkness knoweth not whither he goes. While ye have the light, believe in the light, that ye may be the children of the light."

In Colossians we read, "Giving many thanks unto the Father, which hath made us partakers of the inheritance of the saints in light, who hath delivered us from the powers of darkness and hath translated us unto the kingdom of His son." In this passage there is a clear indication that there is a place in the light and a place of darkness. He was giving thanks that they are partakes of the inheritance of the saints in light and are delivered from the powers of darkness.

In Matthew we read: "And I say unto you, that many shall come from the west and east, and shall sit down with Abraham, and Isaac and Jacob, in the kingdom of Heaven, but the children of the kingdom (of hell) shall be cast out into outer darkness, there shall be weeping and gnashing of teeth." Here again a reference to heaven and a place of outer darkness. He did not say they would be tossed into a hell of fire and brimstone, but only into the outer darkness.

Matthew also records a parable taught by Christ: "Then said the king to the servants, bind his hand and foot and take him away and cast him into outer darkness; there shall be weeping and gnashing of teeth." And in Matthew, Christ again said, "And cast ye the unprofitable servant into the outer darkness, there shall be weeping and gnashing of teeth." In both these passages the unworthy ones were cast into the outer darkness, *not into a hell of fire and brimstone.*

In Ephesians there is a clear reference to light and darkness: "And have no fellowship with the unfaithful works of darkness, but rather reprove them, for it is a shame even to speak of those things which are done of them in secret. But all things that are reproved are made manifest by the light, for whatsoever doth make manifest is light. Wherefor he saith, awake thou that sleepeth, arise from the dead, and Christ shall give thee light."

And again in Ephesians: "For we wrestle not against flesh and blood, but against principalities, against powers, against the rulers of the darkness of this world, against spiritual wickedness in high places."

You will note that the writer referred to the rulers of the darkness, not of a hell of fire and brimstone.

In 2 Peter it is written: "For if God spared not the angels that sinned but *cast them down to hell and delivered them into chains of darkness*, to be reserved unto judgment . . . to whom the mist of darkness is reserved forever."

Here is a hell of darkness, one that is reserved forever, or eternal darkness. No reference is made to torture, fire, and brimstone.

Jude, describing the works of men symbolically, said: "Woe unto them, for they have gone in the way of Cain and run greedily after the error of Balaam for reward, and perished . . . these are spots in your feasts of charity, when they feast with you, feeding themselves without fear, clouds that are without water, carried about on winds, trees whose fruit withereth, without fruit, twice dead plucked out by the roots, raging waves of the sea, foaming out their own shame, wandering stars to whom is reserved *the blackness of darkness forever.*" No fire and brimstone!

He is describing the sinner, those who do not bear fruit, as being those cast out into the outer darkness, forever.

There are many, many more references, all of which describe heaven as a place of light, under rule of the Light of the World, and hell as a place of darkness, ruled by the Prince of Darkness.

When understanding of the word "hell" is achieved, and when superstition is removed, the Scriptures will not bear out a hell of fire and torture, but they do bear out a hell of darkness. In addition, the Scriptures teach that man is not condemned to hell in the sense that we normally understand condemnation, *But man condemns himself*. Based upon his acts and upon his performance, he brings himself under condemnation as a result of his own free acts. The state of his being after death results from his free choice, for it is he that chooses eternity either in darkness or in the light. We will explore this in depth a little later on.

It cannot be denied that we do experience some of the sensations of hell here on earth, with dark deeds, dark thoughts, and dark emotions, but there is another heaven and hell after death. If heaven and hell were only here on earth then it would, for each individual, last only a lifetime, and upon death that would be the end of it. *If this is true then one should not waste time on religion at all*, but should enjoy this life to the fullest and not waste what precious time he has in the pursuit of salvation.

You will recall in Genesis it was God who created the light: "And God said, let there be light and there was light." He made light available to all who would love Him and seek after light and reject the darkness. If any man shall hate the darkness and love the Light of the World, then he shall have his reward, being judged in accordance with his works, and have everlasting life in the kingdon of light.

Likewise, those who hate the light of the world and follow the Prince of Darkness shall also attain their goal. It is man's free choice and it is he who condemns himself to one or the other. If this be true, then how can we charge God with the responsibility for what he obtains and for the state of his existence after death?

It is up to each man to decide if he will follow the Light of the World or the Prince of Darkness, and once he has made his free election the decision that he makes is not revocable, and he will pass away into the element *of his own free choice*, darkness or light.

This needs no defense, and it is only proper and fitting that if anyone seeks after the Prince of Darkness, if he elects to reject the light and live in darkness, then he is most assuredly entitled to spend eternity in the darkness that he most dearly loved in this life—there, perhaps, never to see another living soul. In that darkness he might sometimes hear the faint whisper of another lost soul as they pass in the darkness. There he will wander forever in the never-ending vastness of the darkness which he so dearly loved. Perhaps sometimes he might see far off the faint glow of the light he so willingly rejected, but he has banned himself from that light, he is a victim of his own folly, his own choice, by exercise of his own free will.

Consider that most evil deeds are committed in the darkness. Nightclubs are darkened, bars are dimly lit, most crime occurs in dark streets and in dark alleys. They work behind closed doors, plot their evil deeds behind locked doors with shades drawn to keep out the light. If one elects to live a lifetime in this manner and loves it, why should he not be rewarded in accordance with his desire and loves? Does this need any justification?

But when we look at those who follow the Light of the World, their deeds are done in the open, their meeting places are light and airy. Sometimes they meet upon the mountain top, in early morning, standing open and unashamed before God and the world, their faces bright with hope. They love the light and the truth and they hate that which is dark and the deeds of those who do their work in darkness.

The Christian may fear death because of the of the uknown, but he does not fear God from the standpoint of punishment because he knows that he will get no more than that which he himself bargained for. They have no fear of some supernatural power. They do not fear God because they fear his punishment, but their fear comes from a belief and understanding that one will gain what one seeks, light or darkness. This is the fear a Christian has, a fear of his own weakness. *He does not fear God's strength.* If one rejects the light and elects to find pleasure in the darkness, then he knows that he earned his just reward, and it is this he fears. The Christian prays for strength to follow after the Light of the World and to resist the Prince of Darkness. He does not pray to be protected from the judgment of God, for he knows that he is judged by his own acts and works and that it is he who sits as judge by his own acts and works and that it is he who sits as judge and jury upon his own life and commits his own soul to one or the other, light or darkness.

Jesus said to the Christians in the Sermon on the Mount: "Ye are the light of the world. A city that is set on a hill cannot be hid. Neither do men light a candle and put it under a bushel, but on a candlestick, and it giveth light unto all that are in the house. Let your light so shine before men, that they may see your good works and glorify your Father which is in Heaven." And He also said, "The light of the body is in the eye, if therefore thine eye be single, thy whole body shall be full of light. But if thine eye be evil, thy whole body shall be full of darkness, if therefore the light that is in thee be darkness, how great is that darkness? No man can serve two masters, for either he will hate the one and love the other, or else he will hold to one and despise the other. You cannot serve God and mammon."

Can we support what we have been saying about man condemning himself to eternity in darkness? Listen to what Christ said: "For God so loved the world that He gave His only begotten Son, that whosoever believeth in Him should not perish, but have everlasting life. For God sent not His son into the world to condemn the world, but that the world through Him might be saved. He that believeth on Him is not condemned, but he that believeth not is condemned already, because he hath not believed in the name of the only begotten Son of God. And this is the condemnation, that light is come into the world, and men loved darkness rather than light, because their deeds were evil. For everyone that doeth evil hateth the light, neither cometh to the light, lest his deeds should be reproved. But he that doeth truth cometh to the light, that his deeds may be made manifest, that they are wrought in God.'' Can anything be clearer?

Please note that He said that He did not come into the world to condemn the world, but to save the world and he who believes in Him is not condemned, but he who does not believe in Him is already condemned. This is what I have been trying to make clear, God loves the world, He sent His Son into it not to condemn, but to save. We condemn ourselves by loving darkness and doing dark deeds. If one loves the darkness he is already condemned, but Christ is the Light of the World and tries to bring men into the light. If men reject it, then there is no alternative but to let them have their darkness. How, then, can there by anything to fear from such a God, one who does all He can, has done all He can, and will do all He can to bring men into the light; *shall we fear such a God?* If there is anything to fear it is fear of oneself, of one's weaknesses, of one's rejection of the light and acceptance of the darkness.

Christ also said: "I am come a light into the world, that whosoever believeth on Me should not abide in darkness. And if any man hears my words, and believeth not, I judge him not, for I came not to judge the world, but to save the world."

Is this the God that we are supposed to worship out of fear? Is this the God who will condemn us to a place of hellfire and damnation? He offers us light; if we accept, we are His, if we reject Him we are possessed by the Prince of Darkness. There is an agony in what men charge to God. The blame they place on Him is unjust and unwarranted. If men would only study the word of God and not heed the rantings of confused and immoral men, then truth would prevail, not falseness.

John, in Revelation, describes the Light of the World in his description of the New Jerusalem at the end of time: "And I saw a new Jerusalem . . . and I saw no temple therein, for the Lord God Almighty and the Lamb are the temple of it. And the city had no need of the sun, neither of the moon, to shine in it, for the glory of God did lighten it, and the Lamb is the light thereof, and the nations of them which are saved shall walk in the light of it."

What of those who have not been saved? Then the outer darkness belongs to them, for they will not stand in the light and *they fall heir to the promises of the Prince of Darkness.*

But we Christians need not fear because Christ gave us this promise: "I am the light of the world, he that followeth me shall not walk in darkness, but shall have the light of life."

XIX

Redemption

The word "redemption" means the act of redeeming, or the state of being redeemed, or repurchased, as of something sold; recovery by payment; ransom, as of prisoners, slaves or captured goods; deliverance from sin and its consequences through the sacrifice or atonement of Jesus Christ.

Within the meaning of the word, then we are under Satan's influence and we stand under sin, condemned under the law, *but Christ redeems us, or repurchases us*; we were His, we were lost, and He repurchased us and the ransom demanded was His life, which He paid for our deliverance from sin and sets us free from the law of sin and death.

The word "salvation" has a slightly different meaning, for salvation is the act of saving or delivering, or the state of being saved or delivered from the power and penalty of sin, restored to our former condition prior to our fall into sin.

Thus, the terms "redemption" and "salvation" are closely related. Salvation is the basic and broader word, referring to the condition of men who have been rescued to their place in God's world. Redemption is the process by which the restoration occurs. The real act of Jesus was to free men from bondage to the law of sin and death and the process was by redemption, the giving of Himself as a sacrifice for the sins of the whole world.

When one truly knows that he has been saved from the law of sin and death, that he has been redeemed, or taken away from the ownership of Satan, then he feels impelled to tell others and to be concerned about them, lest they, too, are claimed by Satan.

No follower of Christ can be satisfied with ensuring his own salvation; if this were so, then it would be a selfish religion, but instead he finds himself concerned about other men. The disciples were not satisfied for their own salvation, but put the welfare of others before their own. To them this was all-important and the true mark of one who has been redeemed.

John wrote that Christ said, "A new commandment I give you, that you love one another; even as I have loved you, that you also love one another."

Paul wrote in Romans, "We who are strong ought to bear with the failing of the weak, and not to please ourselves, let each of us please his neighbor for his good, to edify him," and in 1 Corinthians we read: "If one member suffers, all suffer together. If one member is honored, all rejoice together."

In Galatians we are instructed: "Brethren, if a man is overtaken in any trespass, you who are spiritual should restore him in the spirit of gentleness. Look to yourself, lest you, too, be tempted. Bear one another's burdens, and so fulfill the law of Christ. For if anyone thinks he is something when he is nothing, he deceives himself. But let each one test his own work, and then his reason to boast will be in himself alone and not in his neighbor. For each man will have to bear his own load. Let him who is taught the word share all good things with him who teaches. Do not be deceived; God is not mocked, for whatever a man sows, that will he also reap. For he who sows to his own flesh will from the flesh reap corruption, but he who sows to the Spirit will from the Spirit reap eternal life. And let us not grow weary in well-doing, for in due season we shall reap, if we do not lose heart. So, then, as we have opportunity, let us do good to all men, and especially to those who are of the household of faith."

And in Philippians: "Let each of you look not only to his own interest, but also to the interest of others."

These all extol us to live in fellowship.

If there is ever a place where people should feel wanted and secure and loved, it ought to be in the church, for it is here that the redemptive fellowship should be alive and vibrant. *This is not always so.* There are many churches which are cold and impersonal. Concern for one's fellows is one of the great miracles of the redeemed. Paul even urged Christians to avoid anything that would endanger the faith of weaker members, extolling us to avoid anything that is a hindrance to others. He wrote, in part, the following, taken from the fourteenth chapter of Romans: "As for the man who is weak in faith, welcome him, *but not for disputes over opinions.* One believes he may eat anything, while the weak man eats only vegetables. Let not him who eats despise him who abstains, and let not he who abstains pass judgment on he who eats, for God has welcomed both. None of us lives to himself, and none of us dies to himself. If we live, we live to the Lord, and if we die, we die unto the Lord, so then whether we live or die, we are the Lord's. Why, then, do you pass judgment on your brother? Decide never to put a stumbling block or hindrance in the way of a brother. Let us then pursue what makes for peace and for mutual upbuilding. We who are strong ought to bear with the failing of the weak, and not to please ourselves, let each of us please our neighbor for his good, to edify him. Welcome one another, therefore, as Christ has welcomed you, for the glory of God."

The true redemptive fellowship does not extend merely to the membership of a church, but should extend to all the world. *One cannot leave the world behind him when he enters the church and then return to it and take up where he left off.* We cannot have fellowship here and then return home and hate our neighbors. Peter wrote in Acts: "Truly I perceive that God shows no partiality, but in every nation anyone who fears Him and does what is right is acceptable to Him." Everyman is the object of the redeeming love of Christ and must therefore become of concern to the Christian.

This is also true of the church; she cannot minister to the members on Sunday and then turn her back upon the world for the rest of the week. Howard Grimes, a Methodist minister and educator, said: "As we view the church today, we cannot help being struck by its inadequacies as a redemptive fellowship. We are divided into denominations, and denominations are divided into race and class churches. Individual local churches often are torn by inner strife. Much of our activity is pointness and this reflects the poverty of our inner life. The superficiality of much of our church life reveals the inadequacy of our faith."

These are harsh words but there is hope, for there appears to be growing in the church an awareness of a need for a new relationship between groups. Race and class barriers are being torn down and an area of fellowship is spreading. There is a story about a speaker who was an expert on race relationships who criticized the people for failing to acknowledge that Christ loves black people just as much as He does white people and the response was, "Yes, but you ought to have been here five years ago. We couldn't even have had this meeting." This, of course, is meant to point up how foolish we are sometimes in our profession of faith and belief in God's unfailing love for all men who come to Him regardless of race, or color, or background.

The church is beginning to show compassion and understanding for the alienated and the maladjusted. Persons are being accepted into the church in spite of personal and social problems. The alcoholic, the neurotic, the victim of temporary lapses of moral behavior, all are taking up more and more concern of the church. No longer do many churches devote full time to paying members, to the high and mighty, but are welcoming the lowly, the meek, and the weak. Oppositions are still being voiced by the bigwigs of many churches that this or that party shouldn't be admitted because they are just nobody and their presence is not good for the church. We are all aware of the fact that sometimes a church facility is abandoned and a new one built because the class of people who started coming did not suit the taste of the existing membership. *This is the redemptive fellowship?*

Until the church and its members are willing to stand up and fight for the worth of all men, then all human values and worth will continue to decline. We turn to dope, to whiskey, to lusts of the flesh, when we feel that there is nothing to this life, that we are not liked because we dress or wear our hair differently, or our skin is different, or because we dare suggest change. We wonder at our own worth when we are rejected by society because some of our beliefs are different. We grow bitter when we hear of God's love and of the wondrous thing of being a Christian and then we are not welcome in their churches because we are different. Redemptive fellowship is possible only when the worth of *all men* is truly believed and *all men* are welcome and we love one another.

We have been silent too long about the wrongs that we do to our fellows. We have become masters at the art of self-justification and self-vindication. We trust no one for we have suffered hurts because of trust.

We are afraid of making a false decision so we speak in riddles rather than risk the finger of accusation. We need honest men, strong men and women, not the brain trusts, the authority, the theologians, but honest, straight forward people who are willing to speak out and prove the adequacy of our religion and who hold to a simple, uncomplicated belief that Christ died for us that we might have life and He died for all men, not just for the select few, for this is the meaning of the true redemptive fellowship.

Sometimes I think we die too soon when there is so much that we can still do, and we fail to perform our Christian duties to our fellow man, but we should until we, too, are at last felled by the hand of death.

What are some of the prices that we must pay for fellowship? Well, first, it will probably be charged that we act upon the behalf of our fellowman for self-interest, that we seek self-glorification, that we really don't care for our fellow man, that we are do-gooders and busybodies, that we are trying to be smart alecks, that we are trying to make someone else look bad, etc., etc. All we can do is overlook such charges, and it is really quite easy to do so *because these charges are always made by the rabble rousers and by those who protest decency and honor and love.* We must brush aside those barbs and realize that true nobility arises from and grows on self-sacrifice and in those who know a sense of duty and love for his fellow man. How easy it is to point the finger of criticism at those who flow against the tide of life because they refuse to yield to its pressures or to conform to its set of rules that have no foundation upon the ethical or moral standards set forth in the Holy Bible. We are a thorn in their side because we cause them to wonder and to think, when it is much more pleasant to conform and yield our principles so as to gain acceptance by our society.

Well, if we have ears we had better listen, not to the words of the worldly wise but to the small still voice that prods us to do what we know is right and if we are branded as religious fanatics or religious nuts, of what matter is this when we look at the alternatives? The word "fanatic" means, "possessed by a diety or supernatural agent, an unreasoning enthusiast or zealot, in religious or other affairs. Possessed by a diety or the like." *Jesus was a fanatic!* He was surely possessed by the love of God and He was such a fanatic about His love for man that He gave His life that they might live. To be possessed by Christ is the highest aim of the Christian, it is the end result of all that he strives for.

We need never be ashamed of our good works, or our beliefs, nor ever fear the accusing finger of those who would belittle us. It is not easy; being a Christian is difficult, no one ever said it would be easy, but Christ said in Mark: "If any man would come after me, let him deny himself and take up his cross and follow me. For whoever would save his life will lose it; and whoever loses his life for my sake and the Gospel's will save it. For what does it profit a man, to gain the whole world and forfeit his life? For what can a man give in return for his life? For whoever is ashamed of me and my words in this adulterous and sinful generation, of him will the son of man also be ashamed, when he comes in the glory of his Father with the holy angels."

To sum up, when we accept Christ, truly accept Him, we are saved from the law of sin and death and Christ redeems us from the claim that Satan has upon us, and we are set into the temple wall as a building block for the house of God, and we have fellowship with Him, for we are members of His household, thereafter we cannot do other than good works for our fellow men, out of love, and out of a genuine desire to have fellowship with them.

XX

Mysticism

God, speaking in Micah, said, "And I will cut off witchcraft out of thine hand, and thou shalt have no more soothsayers."

We shall use the words "familiar spirits" and "divination." When the expression "a consultor with familiar spirits" is used in the Bible, it means one who speaks to the dead.

"Divination" means one who foresees or foretells events or discovery of hidden knowledge. In the Bible the word is used to also mean one who uses false systems for ascertaining the Divine Will.

This chapter is to apply basically to the consideration of mediums, fortune tellers, concept therapy, astrology, spiritualism, soothsayers, witches, and dream interpreters, and their fellow travelers. What is said here should not be carried beyond those ideologies, nor should any interpretations which would apply to the recognized sciences which pertain to the human mind be made. The words "mystic" or "soothsayer," when used, are usually lumped together.

Many of the above described so-called "arts" are growing in acceptance and, in some cases, are being accepted as religions and the usage of such terms is now being used in everyday language by almost everyone. To say that to delve into such matters does not create an air of excitement and mystery would be false. One develops all kinds of strange and weird feelings, and in many cases a feeling of fear or awe, for associated with all these things are certain unknowns and unexplainable happenings, coincidences, and hallucinations.

A few years ago, before we became so sophisticated, we used the terms voodoo, black magic, black arts, witchcraft, and primitive beliefs in lieu of modern-day terms. *The similarity is, however, startling.* The meaning is the same, for they all have something in common. All deal in the area of supernaturalism and draw upon the unobservable universe as a source of authority. Any interpretations placed upon their experiences, such as the interpretation of dreams, has as much validity and substance as any other interpretation that might be placed upon them, for they are without authority! All have the audacity to state that things unknown and not understood are now known and within the realm of human understanding and, if not understood, nevertheless usable and capable of being presented as fact, and some even identify their activities as religions or, at the least, worthy of incorporating into existing religions.

There is no all-inclusive definition of the word "religion," but basically it means that for a thing to become a religion it must include a beleif in supernatural or mysterious powers, and this belief is associated with feelings of awe, fear, and reverence, and expresses itself in overt activities designed to deal with those powers. Religion is not a mere process of meditation about life and man's destiny, *but the key is that is must provide a means of preserving man's highest values of life.* Anything that degrades this objective cannot be held to be a religion.

Primitive man tended to endow nature with life and to ascribe personalities to their functions. Thus, the worship of the sun gods, the rain gods, or the god of the forest, etc. These became supernatural powers and he assigned to them, in his mind, a form or identify so he would be able to communicate with them. We have heard the expression that we are created in the image of God, *but every man creates an image of God in his own mind!* Primitive man also ascribes great power to deceased ancestors and hence practiced ghost worship and, of course, those who were most proficient in contacting them later became their witch doctors, or high priests.

Primitive man, being exposed to the unknown and to nature, faced with things not understood and with a need to add substance to his existence and justification for his being, founded his beliefs, his gods, his witch doctors, and his pagen rituals. Their ceremonials are ridiculed today by the so-called 'enlightened." Yet, the similarity of practice by moderns to the primitives is worthy of comparison. The primitive and the soothsayer of today both inquired into things not understood and into the unknown and, as a result of their inquiry, will arrive at a belief founded upon no evidence or basis of fact, but upon things imaginary and unreal, add to it their independent interpretation, claim that some god or unknown power revealed the truth to them, find followers, and establish a cult.

The practitioners of voodooism will use a wax doll as a material substance through which the spirits can operate whenever one desires to cast a spell upon his victim. The modern spiritualists will use a trumpet through which the spirit can be contacted and both the primitive and spritualist will, with dogmatism, argue that they practice a legitimate ritual endorsed by some mystical authority whose existence they loudly proclaim and extol, yet whom they have never seen nor spoken to. Both enjoy performing their rituals in darkness or in semi-darkness around a campfire, and they love to use the trance in the performance of their skills. They call their dreams "visions" and proclaim that they are divinely inspired. They call upon the dead and speak in gibberish and announce to their followers that it is a special gift from the unknown, and claim that they have divine sanction for their practices, *yet the law of Moses forbade the consultation of magicians and soothsayers upon pain of death.*

Modern practitioners, while scoffing at the primitive, state that they have sensitive minds and that they are endowed with highly receptive abilities and gifts not available to other mere mortals. They claim that they can communicate with the dead, that they can leave their bodies and travel through time and space and converse with the living and that their dreams have great and profound significance. They interpret the slightest everyday occurrence as having some mystic and wondrous connotation. They have vivid imaginations and at the same time *are incapable of separating fact from fiction.* They operate from the trance, which is nothing more than auto-suggestion or self-hypnosis, which can, with training, be accomplished by anyone, mystic or not, or by hallucinating drugs!

Why have so many people become so eager to participate in these exercises in futility? Why are the exponents of the "arts" receiving such acclaim and acceptance? Has religion failed to give mankind doctrines upon which he can stand? Is there substance to their doctrines, or is it a throwback upon the primitives who attributed all things not understood to a spirit or to some supernatural power? Shall we divert from the course of Christianity and disguise it in supernaturalism and seek after a new god *and shall we call this new god "the human mind"?* Contemplation of the matter will cause one to come to the inevitable conclusion that the practice of the so-called "arts" is a regression into the dark ages, a return to the primitive, and that it is an experiment in potential disaster!

The Bible says, "There shall not be found among you anyone that shall make his son or his daughter to pass through fire, or that shall useth divination, or an observer of times, or an enchanter, or a witch, or a charmer, or a consultor with familiar spirits, or a wizad, for all that do these are an abomination unto the Lord." What does "abomination" mean? *Extreme disgust and hatred, detestation, loathing.* This is strong language, and I sincerely hope you will remember this passage.

The practitioners point with pride to their accomplishments and "successes." They have located lost items, they have located missing persons, described things they never saw, prescribed cures, etc. What is it all about? It is the result of the application, whether conscious or unconscious, of the law of averages, the law of possibility, or probability, and the law of chance. They result from vivid imaginations resulting from what one would expect to see in a given place, environment, city, home, era or time. They are predictions of things and events that have *always* happened and will *always* continue to happen in the universe and in the affairs of men.

David made fun of them when he was asked to interpret the dreams of King Nebuchadnezzar, for he said to him, "The secret which the King hath demanded, cannot the wise men, the astrologers, the magicians, the soothsayers show unto the King?'' Then he continued, ''But there is a God in heaven that revealeth secrets and maketh known what shall be in the latter days.''

Saul did what he could to drive them out of the country of Israel. But for all this, many were still to be found, and the Israelites were always addicted to this sort of superstition. But even Saul himself, after he fell from grace, consulted one of them.

Many of the mystics of today deal in the past. The doctrine of reincarnation is rapidly becoming an accepted theory by many. The exponents of this doctrine take the hypothesis that as a result of their having been reincarnated they have the ability to reveal events of the past. They convey the idea that their former intelligence is carried forward from generation to generation and that during each lifetime they gain greater perfection and assimilate additional knowledge. This theory is expounded upon by some persons that state that they have lived several lives, *and yet many are actually mentally incompetent by any standard that we use to measure intelligence.* Some of them can barely read or write and seem completely devoid of any reasoning power at all. The exponents neglect to advise that knowledge of past history and events can also be obtained by the mere reading of history books and by studying scientific papers and the findings of past thinkers. It does not take supernatural powers to read and to learn what has happened in the past in the course of mankind. One does not need to seek the counsel of the soothsayer to learn of past events. It is available, in book form, to anyone who seeks after knowledge, and most assuredly in one's own mind as to what he has done and seen during his own past life.

The faces of the people who believe in reincarnation will brighten as they say, ''During one of my lives I traveled across the desert in a covered wagon and fought the Indians.'' They are exicted about this great revelation. But no satisfactory answers are given to the following questions: What profound knowledge did you carry forward to this new life? What single truth did you bring to reveal to mankind so he might improve his lot? Nothing? Then of what value is it? Of what value is it if you lived a thousand lives and bring forth no great revelation? Surely these people, while they were in the beyond, where all knowledge is revealed, all truths made know, surely they learned something of value. *Why do they return to earth in search for more knowledge?* Oh, they say, so that the soul can purify itself and grow. Well, having lived and died and witnessed all knowledge and then to return to purify the soul seems kind of stupid to me, because they know— because they've been there—that there is eternal life, *and yet they continue to live in sin!* Even though they have returned three or four times they still gamble on eternal life? Does the soul learn slowly, and if it cannot remember the past or its experiences in the beyond, then how can it purify itself, having no remembrance of the past? Something is missing; of what value is multiple life if nothing is retained from the past life except fighting Indians?

It is impossible for man to conceive a state of not being. You are, how can you not be? As a result, certain Asiatic religions did not conceive of a life in the hereafter but reasoned out a doctrine of evolution or reincarnation. This is understandable, but why does an educated, enlightened, intelligent man who already has a religion which offers eternal life take the position that a better way to achieve immortality is not to follow Christ, but to return to the world over and over again?

A medium, a fortune teller, or an astrologer will, when giving a reading, devote at least ninety percent of the sitting to the telling of past events. Who you are, what you are, what has happened in your lives, lost loves, old disappointments, etc. Of what value is this? To be told of that which you are already aware of is a complete waste of time. The mystics can, by merely applying the law of averages, tell persons what has happened in their past lives, for all things happen at all times and persons are bound to be caught up in some of the happenings. We have all known death, we all suffered illnesses, had disappointing love affairs, made bad business judgments, and all the rest, and conversely we all have known periods of health, success, taken trips, fallen in love, etc. Of what value is this to be told what we already know? If there is no value, why pursue it and squander our valuable time? *We all have hindsight!*

Then we have the mystics that deal in the future. Predictions of earthquakes, fires, storms, deaths, assassinations, illnesses, money, trips we will take, and on and on. The predictions pour out from the mystics, so many that some of them are bound to happen. If the prediction occurs, great praise is given; if they do not occur, then it is said that they cannot be one hundred percent correct because there are always outside influences at work which interfere and prevent infallible predictions. Here, again, the application of the law of averages and possibility will result in the foretelling of events to come with some success. Events have always occurred and they will continue to occur and there will always be some people who will be involved in these happenings and some mystics who will take credit for predicting that it would happen. The very course of human endeavor will foretell certain events; for example, wars can be predicted with fairly good accuracy by any student of history. Earthquakes and fires will most assuredly occur, foretold or not, and if foretold, what can be done to prevent them from happening? If the answer is nothing, then of what value is the prediction? *A thing predicted must come about because if one acts to prevent it from happening then the prediction was false because it did not happen.*

We can predict that we will probably expand our travel in space. We might well establish a base on the moon and men might live there. Inventors can foretell the need for their inventions. Men of medicine can foretell coming epidemics and can prepare for the future. Men foresaw the need for laws, and passed them, for the future. Are these mystics? Is the use of the intelligence and imagination a mysterious and wondrous thing?

The human body will cure itself in many cases without medical aid. If the soothsayer prescribes a salve or ritual and the body heals, can it be said with any certainty that it would not have done so in any event? Even the witch doctor prescribes the use of herbs and potions with a good degree of apparent success. Men of religion saw the need for moral law and for ethical rules of conduct; are they, too, soothsayers? If one knows the background, personality traits, and training of another person, he can foretell with a great deal of accuracy how that person will react to any given situation. Is that, too, a wondrous thing?

Try to pin down the seer to tell the time of a happening and he will state that there is no time, or he will say soon, or in the next few weeks, or years. They always allow themselves plenty of latitude.

The passage of time will erase from the memory many things that are foretold and which do not occur and the mystic is not held accountable for these predictions, for they are forgotten; but if a thing foretold does come about, then it is recalled to vivid memory and no regard is given to the passage of time. Herein lies the greatest success of the medium—the application of the law of averages and the law of possibilities and the reliance upon the forgetfulnsss of the recipients of their predictions with the passage of time.

All persons look into the future, they plant seed with the view of a harvest, they build dams, they irrigate land, they purchase insurance, they enact social security, they build schools, offices, churches—all designed to take care of the present and possible expansion, the future. Are these things of another world or simply the reliance upon common sense?

Persons with highly developed imaginations and with strong desires and hopes will permit predictions to become so vividly implanted in their minds that when they do happen they attribute them to something supernatural. The fact that they came about through planning or as a result of their having been in the right place at the right time and under the right conditions to have caused them to happen is completely ignored and no consideration given thereto. Most people accept the prediction as a fact of life, but the mystic says that the event was revealed to him. Any person, having a situation to face, will weigh the matter in his mind and come to a conclusion that this or that will be the result and act accordingly. He will, however, normally drop the matter there and go his way, but not the mystic, for he states that all happened because God gave him a vision and he abided by it and caused the event to happen.

The future should be responded to by common good sense and one should not rely upon the mystic for guidance because *we all have foresight.*

Many of the mystics are proficient in contacting the dead and the practice of communicating with the dead is becoming quite commonplace. Well, the primitives put great stock in their ancestral ghosts which they believed were endowed with superhuman powers and they believed that their ghosts could manipulate human and natural occurrences. They believed that if they placated them with gifts and offerings that they would respond in a favorable way and act in their behalf. Thus, the primitives communicated with their ancestral ghosts and acted in accordance with the messages they received from the spirit world. *Modern mystics make the same claims!* The so-called messages from the dead are so shallow that they form a source for pure humor. "This is Uncle Ned; it is very beautiful over here. Your Aunt Martha is here with us. We are worried about you, do not take that trip you have planned." Or, "This is Uncle John. Do not be sad for us; it is wonderful here. We are well and happy, please be careful." Why would they want them to be careful and why would they worry about them? If things are so great, I would think that they would try to speed up the reunion.

There has never been a single report that the dead ever said, "I saw God today. I cannot describe the wonders of it. He spoke to me and explained many things to me, but you would not understand; but I can tell you this, He is truly a God of love." Nor have any of them said, "I met Jesus face-to-face for the first time this morning. What a wonderful experience. He is all that we have been told that He is. Tell the people to believe." The only messages that we receive are shallow, hollow words. Surely the most important things one would tell would be of the wonders of God and Jesus, of the glory of God, of the wonders of heaven. Surely they would tell the great truths that mankind searches after. *Well, even the mystics are intelligent enough to fear damnation for such outlandish falsehood, and will not risk damnation when they convey the messages from the dead.*

What folly! The mysteries of the universe, of the heavens, of the unknown, are available to the dead and yet they are reluctant to reveal these things to the living. And isn't it incredible that the dead, with all these wonders, are loathe to leave this world, but ignore these wonders and linger to talk to the living? The mystics accomplish nothing by talking to the dead, they render no service to mankind, there are no great revelations, no great truths come forth, only that Aunt Martha is well and happy. *The foolishness of this claim is so lacking in common sense and logic that one must wonder about the reasoning powers of those who claim they can contact the dead.*

Haven't you ever wondered about the poor souls who hear voices in the night, who contact the dead, who attach all manner of significance to dreams, who see shapes and flying trumpets? Many are good-intentioned people, although not necessarily harmless, for they teach their hallucinations as fact to the weak-minded and to the foolish and lead them down paths of false beliefs! The sin they commit is awesome, for they destroy the search for God-given knowledge.

In the third chapter of Jeremiah we read the following:

"Woe be unto the pastors that destroy and scatter the sheep of my pasture! saith the Lord. Ye have scattered my flock, and driven them away, and have not visited them; behold, I will visit upon you the evil of your doings, saith the Lord.

And I will gather the remnant of my flock out of all countries whither I have driven them, and will bring them again to their folds; and they shall be fruitful and increase. And I will set up shepherds over them, which shall feed them; and they shall fear no more, nor be dismayed, neither shall they be lacking, saith the Lord.

Behond, I am against the prophets, saith the Lord, that use their tongues, and say, He saith. Behold, I am against them that prophesy false dreams, saith the Lord, and do tell them, and cause my people to err by ther lies, and by their lightness; yet I sent them not, nor commanded them; therefore they shall not profit this people at all, saith the Lord.

Therefore behold, I, even I, will utterly forget you, and I will forsake you, and the city that I gave you and your fathers, and cast you out of my presence; and I will bring an everlasting reproach upon you, and a perpetual shame, which shall not be forgotten.''

Here is a clear indictment of apostasy! To apostatize is to abandon or desert the principles of faith to which one previously adhered. *To fall away from or to depart from the faith is to apostatize.* Timothy warns us, "Avoid such people, for there are those who will listen to anyone and can never arrive at a knowledge of truth, they oppose the truth, men of corrupt mind and counterfeit faith."

Luke describes apostates as those who hear, receive the word with joy, but have no root; for a while they believe, but in time of temptation they fall away.

Timothy also says, "Now the Spirit speaketh expressly, that in latter times some shall depart from the faith, giving heed to seducing spirits and doctrines of devils."

In Hebrews we find the following warning: "Take heed, brethren, lest there be in any of you an evil, unbelieving heart, leading you to fall away from the living God."

Assent to the teachings of mystics does not produce a fruit-bearing faith, and therefore cannot be a saving faith, and as such has no place in the life of a Christian.

The Bible says, "But understand this, that in the last days there will come times of stress. For men will be lovers of self, . . . lovers of money, . . . proud, arrogant, abusive, . . . disobedient to their parents, ungrateful, unholy, inhuman, inplacable, slanderers, fierce, haters of good, treacherous, reckless, swollen with conceit, lovers of pleasures rather than lovers of God, holding to the form of religion but denying the power of it."

Mystics are so motivated for profit and for fame that they will put forward any doctrine that might find a few dolts who will spend their money.

The disciples believed that these people were possessed by demons, *Yet now we give them honor!*

"And it came to pass, as we went to prayer, a certain damsel possessed with a spirit of divination met us, who brought her masters much gain by soothsaying. But

Paul turned and said to the spirit, 'I command thou in the name of Jesus Christ to come out of her,' and he came out that same hour and when her masters saw that their hope for their gains were gone they charged us.''

The ability to talk to the dead through dreams, to invisible souls, dates back to the primitive. Suppose he dreamed of a hunting expedition which resulted in his bringing back game and enjoying a fine dinner. Upon awakening he found, of course, that he had never left his abode. How could he explain this except through the belief in a spiritual self which is separable from his bodily self and which can lead an independent existence? Death, halucinations, shadows, and echoes were other factors leading to this belief in spirits. He began to rationalize that if his spirit could contact other spirits through dreams then he could be led to successful hunts, etc. Thus if he followed the dream, and it worked out, then he interpreted it correctly. If he failed, then wrongly.

The mystic lives in a never-never land of childish dreams and then asks others to join in his world of fantasy. The mystics say that the power of the human mind is untapped, but they deny logic. It is untaped, but in the understanding of things real, not in things not understood. They say the mind can understand all things, but they counsel us not to believe that which is reasonable. In one's search for a greater meaning to life he should not look to ghosts, to shapes, to trumpets, to misty shrouds, but should seek knowledge and reason and to things that can be relied upon. *He should turn away from the voices of dead men to the voices of living men. He should listen to the spirit of God, not to the ghost of the departed; he should seek not to interpret dreams, but to interpret life. He should not look to the past, but look to the future, borrowing only from the past that which is usable. He should place his destiny not in the dead, but in the living, for there is the hope of the future; he should not substitute the unreal for the real.* Let the dead go and seek life, for as Christ said, "Let the dead bury the dead."

The only authority used in support of the positions is the Holy Bible. When such practices are condemned in passage after passage, and referred to as an abomination unto the Lord, then I must stand upon it. To date, I have discovered no greater authority than the Holy Scriptures and for me it is enough. I do not seek to change your ideas or beliefs, only to point out certain dangers, fallacies, and Biblical doctrine in support thereof. I only hope that whatever you wish to believe will not become an abomination unto the Lord.

XXI

Religion

If the world ever needed religious tolerance, it needs it now. Bigotry and conceit have no place in religion, but common brotherhood, love among all men who must find the way to band together and form a mighty force to combat evil, should be the prime objective of any religion. God has worked in the affairs of man since the beginning, and still works among men today. We must acknowledge that God is what He is, and that He did what He did, for the redemption of man, whether anyone else believes it or not!

Each individual must within himself hear the voice of God calling them home. Man enter one by one into the kingdom of God through the narrow gate of repentance as sheep enter one by one into the fold, each known by his own name. As each of us dies he dies alone, and each of us comes to faith in God and His love. But once coming into faith with God, he cannot do otherwise than seek out fellowship with other believers.

A study of religions of the world reveals that each grows upon its own ground and in accordance with its own dogma and laws. It can be understood only by those who have lived and learned of its essence, and any attempt by outsiders to evaluate, condemn and downgrade its significance to those who believe is bound to end in failure. We as Christians stand upon the Bible, but if there is one thing clear about the Bible it is that it is concerned with a renewal of religion in the world. We must remember that *Christ in the New Testament does not call men to a new religion, but to life.* He offers men life around and apart from the law to which all other religions bind their followers. Christianity offers life through love, acceptance, and belief in Christ, regardless of one's performance under the law.

Christ said that "no man comes unto the Father save by me," and we are inclined to stand smug upon this statement, aloof from other religions, looking down upon all of the other words of God as being inferior to that which we believe. To whom was Christ speaking? He was speaking to those who follow Him and to those Jews who refused to believe in his divinity. Anyone who hears of and knows Jesus Christ and has read of His atonement and rejects Him and elects to stand under law will be bound under law.

132

It is their free choice and if they elect to stand under law they are sure to fail. Those who know Christ and who reject Him cannot go unto the Father *because Christ cannot, under law, intercede for them.* All other religions of the world bind men under law and they are judged under law in accordance with their acts and have no one to intercede for them, and they must therefore rely upon the mercy of God!

We must always guard against smugness and a feeling that we are assured of salvation because of a doctrine, principle or membership in a religious organization. It is a mistake to hold that the only salvation available to the world is through the acceptance of the Christian doctrine of salvation, or to the principle that only we hold the correct doctrine of grace, and that all we have to do is to express a belief in Christ and we shall be saved. *This is a cheap belief and a cheap way of trying to cover our sins*, and, if hidden behind too strongly, can result in a loss of any desire to live Christian lives under the mistaken belief that we are assured salvation by the mere recitation of the words, "I believe in Christ." Throughout recorded history, millions of souls have knelt to pray before their God and it is an audacious position of anyone to pass judgment upon what they do! To do so constitutes the pinnacle of self-adoration!

There are enough problems in working towards salvation without condemning all other faiths as false; we make no claims that we know the will of God, and His purposes, as He works among men and nations. But we are ready, without reservation, to acknowledge that God is what He is and that He did and will do what He can, for the redemption of man. This much we know: through Christ we, as Christians, are saved; as to what happens to other men of other faiths, we leave that to God.

For anyone to say that he knows what God does in the universe and what his designs are reminds me of a story about a man who simply could not understand life. He read all of the wisdoms of the world and still could not understand anything about life. He traveled all over the world, talking to the wise men of the age, and always returned without the answer to the puzzle of life. Then one day he heard about a very wise old lama who lived high on a Tibetan mountain. This man was supposed to be the wisest of the wise men. So the man embarked upon a journey to find this man. At last he came to a small village at the foot of a tremendous mountain, and he inquired of the wise old lama. The villagers comfirmed that indeed there was such a man and that he lived on top of the mountain. He was told that he was wise beyond any man and that he knew the wisdoms of the world. He was told that there was nothing that the lama did not know, for he had spent his entire life in study and meditation and became the wisest of the wise.

The man formed a group to lead him up the mountain. For two days they climbed, and on the evening of the second day, sure enough they could look up and see the lama sitting in front of his stone house, meditating. But the last part of the journey was so steep that the other men refused to go further. The following morning the man proceeded alone and at last, in the late afternoon, he arrived before the lama, tired and exhausted.

He approached the lama and said, "Sir, I understand that you are a man of God, and that you know all things."

The lama replied, "It is true, son, I have learned all there is to know about life. What is it you wish to know?

The man asked, "Sir, what is life?"

The wise old lama gazed off into the distance and it was a full thirty minutes before he replied. Then at last he said, "Life, son, is a stream."

The man looked upon him in amazement, then became angry. He ranted at the lama, "Do you mean that I have traveled halfway around the world at tremendous expense, that I risked my life in climbing this mountain and all you can say is that life is a stream?"

The lama looked at the man in disbelief, then with shock and with panic in his voice he asked, "Do you mean that life is not a stream?"

We know about as much about what God does to sustain His universe as the lama about life. I can, however, talk about God sustaining His word with man, how over the centuries He has tried to teach him how to live in his universe as His children, how He has used great teachers in the past, and how men so many times twist His words and form false religions. This attempt by God to teach men proves His love for that portion of His creation, for He has created nothing like man in all the vastness of the universe. Although we might speculate that there is intelligent life on other planets, to date not one shred of evidence has been brought forward to prove this, and if it should come forward, it would not alter our beliefs. We would hope that He would have greater success with other colonies of men that He may have planted in other parts of the universe than He has had with those He planted on earth. It is impossible to discuss all of the religions of the world in detail but, it can be shown how God works to sustain His word among men.

The leaders of the great religions of the world all taught a good moral life. Almost without exception, the basic moral ideas of not killing, stealing, committing adultery, bearing false witness, together with living the simple life, are stressed in the original presentation of the great religions, but man, in the course of living, injected into them their own doctrines and came up with variations of the basic religion. Merely look at the many denominations in the Christian religion and it is easy to see how this occurs.

The existence of some outside power, or influence, is recognized almost universally by men. The primitives created gods in abundance to explain that which they did not understand. Some of their gods took on human forms, others animals, or combinations of both, and this practice continues well beyond the advent of civilization, as witnessed by the many Greek, Roman, and Norse gods. This belief in multiple gods evolved into finally a single godhead, but often having trinities, as in our case, the Father, Son, and

Holy Ghost. The Egyptians had Osiris, Isis, and Horus, and the Hindus Brahma, Vishnu, and Siva; however, Judaism and Islam retained one God— the Jews say there is one God, and Islam says there is one Allah. Although the Egyptian religion had three godheads, they still included many other gods, being part human and part animal.

Krishna speaks of other religions as follows:

"Whenever there is a decay of righteousness, and there is an exaltation of unrighteousness, then I, myself, come forth, for the protection of the good, for the destruction of evildoers, for the sake of the firmly established righteousness, I am born from age to age. He who thus knows my divine birth and action in its essence cometh to me. Freed from passion, fear, and anger, filled with me, taking refuge in me, purified in the fire of wisdom, many have entered by being. However men approach me, even so do I welcome them, for the path men take from every side is mine."

He also taught these famous words: "I have taught you that wisdom which is the secret of secrets. Ponder it carefully. Then act as you think best." (*Free choice.*) "These are the last words I shall say to you, the deepest of all truths. I speak for your own good. You are the friend I chose and love . . . you must never tell this holy truth to anyone who lacks self-control and devotion or who despises his teacher and mocks at me . . . (Do not case your pearls before swine.) . . . and if any man meditates on this sacred discourse of ours, I shall consider that he has worshipped me in spirit. Even if a man simply listens to these words with faith, and does not doubt them, he will be freed from his sins and reach the heaven of the righteous." (*He whosoever liveth and believeth in me though he be dead yet he shall live.*) "That reality which pervades the universe is indestructible." (*God is,* or *Eternal God.*) "No one has the power to change the changeless." (*God, the allpowerful.*) "Bodies are said to die, but that which possesses the body is eternal." (*Belief in the immortality of the soul.*) "It cannot be limited or destroyed." (*Everlasting life.*)

From all these religions there have been many offspring, taking with them what they wanted, rejecting that which they did not want, and adding to it those things they found compatible. There are so many variations that it would be impossible to even mention them, they exist in all religions, including Christianity. We have touched only briefly upon the basic religions for one purpose, and that is to show how God has been working in the affairs of men since recorded time, trying to show the way to eternal life, and that's what religion is really all about.

So we cannot attempt to tell you how God sustains His creation, but we can state that He sustains His love for mankind, and that throughout history He has from time to time reached down among the masses of men and lifted out men to teach His word. *He loved His creation of mankind so much that He even sacrificed the life of His own Son to this end.* It is certain that what those great teachers taught does not even resemble many of the doctrines being presented by the multitude of sects that have spun off from the original teachings. It is as though the hand of evil reaches down each time the truth is given to crush the spirit of earnest men seeking to learn and to discover the truth, to prevent them from perpetrating those truths, but somehow the basic laws of morality and love survive.

Today it continues in our lives, for many would place less emphasis on religious dogma and place more importance on social values. Many more want to reconcile its doctrines with scientific knowledge. Others teach that it is the supreme worth of man that is important. Others cocnern themselves with rituals more than dogma, and on and on the diversification continues, until in some instances it is impossible to believe that you are in a church professing to be associated with Christianity. The trend towards socialization and secularization of religion is undeniable. Still our Lord continus his relentless search for those who would come to Him, be reunited with Him, and obey His word.

Since recorded history only goes back about 5,000 years, we do not know what preceded it, nor do we know the conditions that man was created in at the beginning, nor how far he has regressed from the state of his creation, before he once more began to rise towards the teachings in the beginning. Nevertheless, it is interesting to note that all societies have had some form of religion which causes one to speculate whether, no matter how far man regressed, he still retained memory and knowledge of life as it was in the beginning. Some of the earliest travelers and missionaries who went to primitive lands reported that they had encountered evidence of tribes that had no religion, but such reports were later shown to have no foundation in fact. This occurred simply because they thought they had no religion, because their beliefs and practices did not correspond to their notion of what a religion must include. Careful studies by students of the primitives have not found any people without beliefs and practices which cannot be said to constitute a religion.

Religion is not only found everywhere, but it also goes back to the earliest times. Authorities maintain that the earliest predecessors of the modern man, the neanderthals, must have had some sort of religion, since there is evidence that they buried their dead in a definite position and placed their tools at their side, indicating a belief in an afterlife.

Religion is a unique institution, for all other institutions can be traced back to the animal needs of man, to his physical characteristics. All of man's social organizations, no matter how much they may differ, are based upon the physical facts of sex, infancy, caring for the young, life in a group and to survival. Even economic organizations are rooted to man's quest for food, shelter, and clothing. It is difficult to ascertain any condition of animal life that demands a religion. As to humanity, it likewise has no conditions that demand a religion, for all moral and ethical codes can be served just as well by laws, by desires of men for admiration, by the desire for acceptance, through the fear of punishment, and by the law of survival.

Man does not need a religion to discover the benefits of morality, he needs only to use common sense. He need only consider the objectives of the society in which he lives, and the individuals who compose it, and he will easily see that virtue is advantageous, and vice disadvantageous to himself and to his society. He can tell his fellow men that to be just, moderate, sociable, kind, and generous need not be laws from God, but should be followed simply because it is pleasurable to do so. Man can tell his fellow men that they need not fear vice and crime because they will be punished in the hereafter, but because they will be punished in this life. Why does man need a doctrine of eternal hell in order to be good when he can see that his greatest interest lies in meriting the esteem and admiration of everyone around him and in abstaining from anything which might cause him to incur the censure, contempt and resentment of his society? Man knows all these things, and he needs nothing more to induce him to live a moral life, *yet there is a desire in the hearts of all men for some form of religion.* What is the origin of this unquenchable desire?

It is held by many that fear of death and fear of the unknown is responsible for religion, and that fear of the natural forces led man to believe in deities who could manipulate nature. Man concluded, therefore, that if the gods could be induced to intervene in his behalf, then all he need do is offer up sacrifices and gifts and appeals and all would be well. But this doesn't hold water, *for it does not explain belief in eternal life*, or the development of ways to attain it.

Research of the history of mankind reveals that he has always had a religion of some form, as though it were implanted long ago at his creation, in true form, and that man in the course of living has lost the truth and still seeks after it. Thus the Garden of Eden, where man knew God and denied His word and was turned out from the Garden and *mankind still seeks, yearns for a return to the Garden*, and in that search God has not turned away but works with men so that they might one day find the way back.

This is why we believe in the statements, "Seek and ye shall find, knock and it will be opened to you," and "nothing is covered that will not be revealed, nor hidden that will not be known."

Throughout history man has sought truth and understanding, and it has been given to him over and over again, but he only perverts it.

Christ, when interpreting the parable of the sower, said: "When anyone hears the word of the kingdom and does not understand it, the evil one comes and snatches away what is sown in his heart, this is what was sown along the path. As for what was sown on the rocky ground, this is he who hears the word and immediately receives it with joy, yet he has no root in himself, but endures for a while, and when tribulation or persecution arises on account of the word immediately he falls away. As for what was sown among thorns, this is he who hears the word, but the cares of the world and the delight in riches choke the word and it proves unfruitful. As for what was sown on good soil, this is he who hears the word, and understands it, he indeed bears fruit, and yields, in one case a hundredfold, in another sixty, in another thirty.''

God has sown His seed of truth over and over and men still do not understand. Those that do are reaped unto His harvest, those that do not die on the vine. Let us always pray that His seeds will, in our case, fall upon the good soil.

XXII

Who Am I?

We have all heard the laments, "Who am I?", "What am I?", and "Why was I created?" We have also heard the plaintive cries which bemoan one's life, such as, "I'm trying to find myself." These are the cries of anguished souls; however, far too often they are the mere mouthings of those who would ape their peers and have no substance at all. Nevertheless, the questions are valid and deserve to be addressed from a Scriptural standpoint.

Christians accept Scripture whenever it pertains to Jesus, but they tend to ignore Scripture when it refers to Satan. But this is an error because one cannot pick and choose which part of Scripture one will accept and which part one will reject. One must either accept all of Scripture or none of it. Partial acceptance is not a satisfactory alternative. The Scriptures were either inspired by God or they were not. *Lack of understanding does not provide grounds for rejecting any part of Scripture.* Most Christians do not like to face the reality of Satan's existence; it does not fit neatly into their preconceived ideas of forgiveness, justice and love.

Most ministers will avoid the subject of Satan because they know that they must placate their flock, and that they must leave people with a good feeling after each sermon if they are to continue to serve. Thus they very rarely address the subject from the pulpit. They know that it is not a popular subject, and besides, it tends to disturb the congregation. The minister knows that if he does not preach that which is pleasing to the congregation, they will demand his resignation and will replace him with a minister who is willing to preach that which makes them comfortable. We should not delude ourselves into believing otherwise, for although we justify what we do using other reasons, the result is the same.

The Scriptures have a great deal to say about the reality of Satan:

"How art thou fallen from Heaven, O Lucifer, son of the morning! How art thou cut down to the ground, which did weaken the Nations! For thou hast said in thine heart, I will ascend into Heaven, I will exalt my throne above the stars of God; I will sit also upon the mount of the congregation, in the sides of the North; I will ascend above the heights of the clouds; I will

be like the most high. Yet thou shalt be brought down to Hell, to the sides
of the pit. They that see thee shall narrowly look upon thee, and consider
thee, saying, is this the man that made the earth to tremble, that did shake
kingdoms; that made the world as a wilderness, and destroyed the cities
thereof; that opened not the house of his prisoners? All the kings of the
Nations, even all of them, lie in glory, everyone in his own house. But thou
art cast out of thy grave like an abominable branch, and as the raiment of
those that are slain, thrust through with a sword, that go down to the stones
of the pit; as a carcass trodden under feet. Thou shalt not be joined with
them in burial, because thou hast destroyed thy land, and slain thy people;
the seed of evildoers shall never be renowned." (Isaiah)

"For God spared not the angels that sinned, but cast them down to hell,
and delivered them into chains of darkness, to be reserved unto judgment."
(11 Peter)

"Ye are of your father the devil, and the lust of your father ye will do.
He was a murderer from the beginning, and abode not in the truth, because
he has no truth in him. When he speaketh a lie, he speaketh of his own:
for he is a liar and the father of it." (John)

"He that committeth sin is of the devil; for the devil sinneth from the
beginning. For this purpose the son of God was manifested, that he might
destroy the works of the devil." (1 John)

"Be sober, be vigilant; because your adversary, the devil, as a roaring
lion, walketh about, seeking whom he may devour." (1 Peter)

"Fear none of these things which thou shalt suffer; behold, the devil shall
cast some of you into prison, that ye may be tried; and ye shall have tribulation ten days: Be thou faithful unto death, and I will give thee a crown of
life." (Rev.)

"And there was war in Heaven: Michael and his angels fought against
the dragon; and the dragon fought and his angels, and prevailed not; neither
was their place found any more in heaven. And the great dragon was cast
out, that old serpent, called the devil, and Satan, which deceiveth the whole
world: he was cast out into the earth, and his angels were cast out with him."
(Rev.)

There are many more references to Satan in the Scriptures, but the foregoing is intended to establish a predicate for the following and to substantiate
many of the statements put forward in the preceding chapters.

It can be seen that there was a conflict in Heaven and a war resulted,
with Satan and his angels ultimately being cast out. However, this left several

questions for all time—for all eternity. What would the universe have been like had Satan and his followers been victorious? What would have happened if God had not destroyed Satan? Why did God fear Satan? Why did God remove Satan and his followers from the Universe? Of what was God afraid? God could have brought his mighty power to bear and could have destroyed Satan and evil forever, but had He done so, the questions would have remained for all time, for all eternity. Throughout eons of time the universe would never know peace, and underlying turmoil would remain forever.

The questions had to be resolved, but to whom shall they be submitted? To delegate this responsibility to the angels would have been inconclusive, for the angels were in possession of all knowledge and were not, therefore, in a position to render an unbiased opinion. *Responsibility for the resolution of the angelic conflict has been delegated to man, and it is he and he alone who will resolve these questions for all time. It is he who must leave no doubt as to his ultimate solution!* This is an awesome charge! It is we to whom the whole universe looks for the ultimate solution of the angelic conflict! When the Prince of Darkness challenged the goodness and greatness of God and then tried to exalt himself above God, the angelic conflict was born. Satan did succeed in deceiving many of the angels who joined him in battle against the angels of God, and the great deceiver has never relented in his struggle to control the minds of men. We can take the never-neverland approach and say that we were created so that God could love us or because God was a lonely God and needed the companionship of man. But this is foolishness. Surely life had a deeper meaning than satisfying the whims of some God. God could have showered his love upon the angels and satisfied his loneliness in their company. Can it be that God found the angels to be boring and unlovable? What nonsense! If resolution of the angelic conflict is not our charge, then our existence has no substance at all, we are of no worth to God, and we are to be the most pitied of all creation!

We must understand that man has been given free choice; it was imperative that he be a free agent so that his decision could never be subject to challenge. Man must be subjected to all that is good and to all that is evil so that when he has rendered his decision in fulfillment of his charge, all of creation will know, for all eternity, that love of God and good are the highest goals to which one can aspire, and that Satan and evil are the lowest goals to which one can aspire.

It should be clear to any man that resolution of the angelic conflict had to be resolved by someone other than the angels. It is this charge that has been given to mankind! It is for this purpose that we were born. It is for this reason that man was created. God gave us life and assigned us a mission that we must not abort in betrayal of the very reason that we were created. Who are you? You are the hope of the universe! Humanity must stand together and unite to oppose Satan and evil in all of its forms until victory is ours. Our charge is an awesome thing and the trust that God has shown in us is unsurpassed in the annals of human history!

But the tragedy is that man's charge has been diluted by Satan, who has caused many to yield to the anti-Christ governments, to the criminals, and to the sinners. *They follow like blind sheep in the footsteps of Satan.* They have buried their heads in the proverbial sand and they say there is no evil. Some who profess love of man and God have become radicals, terrorists and zealots, and the sins they commit in doing what they think is a response to the will of God is greater than the sin they seek to correct! They bomb, burn, maim and kill in the name of God and in support of their misguided beliefs. This is a response to love? What they do defames the love of God and betrays the sacrifice made by Jesus. Their conduct and acts are an abomination unto the Lord and when death calls, they must appeal their case to God's great mercy and forgiveness with heads hanging in shame for what they have done. What God's response will be none can say.

Some put forward a doctrine of meekness and mildness and they go to unbelievable ends to assist the criminal and his fellow travelers. *They would even protect the dope peddlers who are in the process of destroying an entire generation of the young!* They have duped the present generation into believing that drug use is healthful, that the use of mind-destroying hallucinating drugs is a substitute for reality, and that the search for kicks is all that is important. In addition, they believe that Christ taught a doctrine of meekness, but at the same time, they fail to recognize that He taught a doctrine of brotherly love on the basis of one individual towards another individual. *His was a doctrine of individualism.* If every man would but abide by the teachings of Jesus—namely, that we love one another—then there would be no crime, no war between nations, no minds and bodies destroyed by drugs, and all men would thereafter walk in dignity and with self-respect..

Jesus never became embroiled in the law of Caesar, but He taught love— one man for another. Christ never advocated that the thief and the murderer run free among his fellows, robbing and maiming his victims. He never taught that the murderer and the thief be provided with excellent surroundings or that they should be loved and set free, to kill and rob at will, without the intervention of the society of which they were a part. It is axiomatic that any society is only as strong as its determination to enforce the rules that it has established, and that to the extent it does not, it begins to disintegrate; to the extent it does, it remains strong.

That Satan does operate in the affairs of men and nations is substantiated by what Satan offered to Jesus during the temptations. He offered the nations of the world to Jesus, if he would but worship him. "And the Devil took him up, and showed Him all the kingdoms of the World in a moment of time. 'To you I will give all this authority and their glory; for it has been delivered to me, and I will give to whom I will. If you, then, will worship me, it shall be yours.' " It should be obvious to anyone that the Devil could not have so tempted Jesus if he did not have dominion over that which he offered, and that if he had no such authority, then Jesus would have merely mocked him and He would not have responded in the manner in which he did.

How we developed the idea that we should coddle the criminals and all others who break the moral laws of God and the ethical laws of man is in and of itself a mystery. We rush to their aid and all the while claim that we are people of religion. Our legal foundations, politicians, lawyers and courts, particularly our Supreme Court justices, need pause and ask themselves which is more sacred, America and the Constitution, or God and the Holy Scriptures! We love to run about shouting to our fellows and to God, "Hey, look at me, am I not one who loves? Am I not the greatest? See how compassionate I am, how understanding and how loving? I should be rewarded for my good works!" We rush about teaching that the criminal should not be punished, but loved. Then, if this is true, let us love Satan also, for they are his representatives. St. John wrote, "He who commits sin is of the Devil, because the Devil sins from the beginning." We are told that we should blame the environment of one's birth, and not the criminal himself. Nothing prevents the misfits from rising above their environment, and many have done so. These people set themselves above God, as did Satan, in believing that they are more loving, more compassionate, more forgiving and more understanding than is God! It stands in their minds as an indictment of God for His shortcomings! *How they adore themselves for their own goodness!* Some even call upon God as though He were some kind of a servant and expect Him to solve all their problems, most of which are of their own making, and they demand that God give them salvation for their goodness!

If we believe Scripture then God certainly did not adopt such an attitude towards evil and the sinners. *He drowned the entire world*, except Noah and his family, including women, innocent children and babies, because of their sins! He brought death, plagues and diseases upon the Egyptians because of their disobedience! He drowned an entire army in the Red Sea because they did not abide by His will! He turned a woman into a pillar of salt because she looked over her shoulder in disobedience of His instructions! This is a mealy-mouthed, mild and weak response to sin? If one believes in anything at all he must believe that God has, and continues to, fight evil in all of its forms without mercy! Oh, but we wail, God is God and we are but mere mortals. Well, if we are true to ourselves we will admit that what we do is because we believe that we will receive a favorable response from God and be rewarded for our goodness. *We believe that we can buy our way into eternal life* by doing that which we claim to be good works. *In reality what we do is a favorable response to Satan!* If we would assist the sinner and criminal then look to his soul and not to his fleshly needs!

We think that we are being noble beings when we embrace the criminal.

But let us look at the results of our "goodness". As a result of our failure to face evil squarely and call a spade a spade and to engage evil in mortal combat upon its own ground, crime has increased, not diminished! Today murder is commonplace! Rape occurs all day long! Nations are continuously at war! Dope is destroying our children and our nation and it has reduced our will to rise up and combat evil. We continue to divert land to the raising of grapes for the production of wine, to tobacco, to raising plants and herbs for the manufacture of hallucinating drugs, to raising grain and other plants for alcoholic use; all the while our fellows starve by the thousands all over the world. If we would but use this land for the raising of foodstuffs and then share with those who are in need, there would be no starvation, no children with bloated bellies. They say this cannot be done because of economics. Well, divert the military budgets from death to life—then any consideration of economics does not enter into it at all! Reality demands that we face Satan squarely and that we engage evil in a no-quarter battle for the minds of men. We must either engage evil and rise to new heights, or deny it and fall into oblivion. Mankind now stands upon the threshold! Death is rubbing its hands together in anticipation of the harvest!

We not only gamble our lives, but we also gamble our very souls! Anyone who truly loves God and who hates evil will engage Satan in battle, not just for the sake of their own souls, not with a hope of a reward, but in fulfillment of the trust that God has shown in us. We cannot turn our backs and walk away, basking in our own glory!

We cannot claim ignorance because we know the laws of God, we know the difference between that which we hold to be good or evil, and we know right from wrong. It is imperative that we accept our responsibilities and not sit idly by and whine in the hope that somehow God will intercede and do that which we ourselves ought to do. We cannot become so bogged down in conflicting ideologies which confound the minds of men that we cannot see reality. If we accept and face our responsibilities, we will incorporate a new meaning into our lives, a new purpose. We will reject the proposition that we are just a mere grain of sand upon the beach of life. We will come to realize that we are tremendously important to the universe and to God. Let us do away with the cloak of meekness and mildness and draw upon the mighty power of God and stand fast in the face of our adversaries. We must cease engaging in idle prayers and we must stop crying out for God's assistance in matters which we ourselves can resolve, if we will but share with our fellows, and use the God-given talents that we possess. We must use all of our strength, wisdom and abilities in the conflict with Satan and stand ready to do battle against his evil influences. We sing, "Onward Christian Soldiers"—now let us act and fulfill the charge for which we were created!

We must shun those who would tell us that we should abandon the worship of God and turn to the humanities, and in the process support the free swingers, the deadbeats, the criminals, and the bums in high style with our hard-earned tax dollars.

Youth and the sex deviates tell us that free and uninhibited sex will result in happy, healthy people and will end their frustration. Free and open sex is their cry! *The cry has even been taken up by the Church itself!* If engaging in abnormal sex acts, if watching nude men and women commit sexual acts, if engaging in sex with each new person of the opposite sex with which one comes into contact and if living out of wedlock is bringing forth a brand-new world of happiness, then the results must belie themselves. If herpes, A.I.D.S., syphilis, gonorrhea, unwanted pregnancies, child abuse and sexual harassment, broken homes, deserted children and abortions are making a grand new world of sublime happiness, then we must be wrong. But if this is so, then why are there so many tears? As a result of so many tears it appears that there could not be a single drop of water in the oceans of the world that did not at one time slide down some human cheek in the form of a tear as a result of broken dreams attributable to sex. Where is all this promised happiness?

The young and the self-made wise tell us that it is they who have the key to happiness and knowledge, and they offer us a new way of life, a new morality. But the Scriptures say, "Behold the Lord came with His holy myriads to execute judgment on all, on sinners, these are grumblers, malcontents, following their own passions, loudmouths, boasters. It is they who set up divisions, worldly people, devoid of the spirit." As responsible Christians, we must find a way to bring this sexual madness to an end and return to the sane, the good, and the beautiful.

We act as though we are afraid of our children, of making value judgments; yet we cry out to God for his assistance and guidance in rearing our children while we ourselves know what we ought to do.

We cry "Peace, peace," but peace does not come. We hear of our world leaders meeting in attempts to bring an end to war, and in this there is a real tragedy because these men are supposed to be the most intelligent men available from the nations of the world, *and they are supposed to represent civilized people.* Yet they talk about ways of killing each other by methods which are acceptable to all parties! They meet to decide who shall have the most destructive missiles, the most warheads, whether chemical and bacterial warfare is permissible, how many warplanes, tanks, cannons and warships each side should have. This is sheer folly! There will be no peace as long as billions of dollars are diverted by powerful men into the manufacture, purchase and sale of the implements of war. These men do not want peace but war, they do not want love but hate, and they do not want saneness but madness! We have been duped into believing that it is better to spend one hundred million dollars on a warplane which will become obsolete within five years, rather than to spend one hundred million dollars for foodstuffs in order to feed our starving brethren. In both events the money would be obtained through taxation and spent. *One for death and one for life!* But, we wail, war and "defense" spending bolsters the economy and provides jobs. Well, if the nations of the world would divert these huge sums of money from "defense" spending to the raising of foodstuffs, thousands would flock back to the farms in order to share in this bonanza and thousands more would be employed in the processing, storage, transportation and distribution industries. Supplies and farm equipment would be purchased instead of tanks, warplanes and other weapons of war which would, in turn, provide thousands of additional jobs to replace those lost to the "defense" industries. We have confused our priorities and we tax and spend for death instead of for life!

If we act responsibility in the fulfillment of our purposes in this life, and if we will but take up our beds and walk, then we will truly know a new zest for living, a new exaltation of life, and it is then that we will have a new meaning for our lives, a new purpose. It is then that we will come to realize that *we are* truly important to our God, to the groaning universe which awaits our decision, to the angels, and to all mankind. If we will but cease vacillating we will not fail our God, nor will we falter in our charge. If we stop attending to the doctrines of Satan, we can vow to our God that Satan will not placate us, nor will he lull us into a sense of false pride and self-adoration, nor shall we permit Satan to lure us into believing that the humanities are more important than is the love of God or that a lie is as good as is the truth. *We must not permit ourselves to be deluded into becoming more fearful of the atom bomb than of the coming wrath of God, whose patience will not always prevail.*

All men of religion, no matter of what faith, must band together and rise up, Jew and Gentile, Hindu and Moslem, black man and white man, red man and yellow man, and form an invincible army against those who would destroy our nobility. Together we must form an army so powerful that the forces of evil cannot prevail against it. We must tell all men of evil hearts that we will no longer permit them to deny us our heritage, that we will no longer permit them to hold us down in the muck of this life while they build their ivory castles and establish their empires with the blood of our youth and the sweat of our brow. We shall tell them that there is no profit to be found in the peddling of sin, death, and destruction.

We must raise the banner of our God, as did our soldiers on Iwo Jima, and engage Satan and his fellow travelers in battle against evil in the fulfillment of our charge, our destiny. When we assume our responsibility and do that for which we were created, it is then that we also fulfill the ultimate will of our God!

You are important to God. If you believe this you will live; deny it and die! The torch is held in your hands. Lift it high with pride, or let it fall and flicker out in the mire. The choice is yours, life or death. Which shall it be?